Praise for *Prayer Revolution*

This book goes for the heart! It also goes quickly, yet deeply, into the real issues facing the church in this critical area of prayer. John Smed has uniquely identified the problems facing the contemporary church, but he also brings biblical ideas and truth so that we journeymen will have a workable tool we can adapt to any group or church. I have seen two crippled churches move quickly to a new focus and practice of prayer.

TERRY GYGER
Coordinator, LiNX

Read this book, and read it again. There are books on prayer, and then there is this one. Filled with prophetic insights distilled from a lifetime spent on the front lines of mission, *Prayer Revolution* is packed with rich theological reflection, careful biblical insights, and practical application. It is not another book on prayer. It is an invitation to another way of living. It is disruptive, as Jesus was; it is timely, as the Spirit always is; it is soul-nourishing and life-changing, as the Father meant it to be. Read it and be changed.

DAN MACDONALD
Senior minister, Grace Toronto Church

Solid and convicting. A biblical call for us to connect with our God.

TOM WOOD
Author, *Gospel Coach*

Prayer Revolution fills an important gap, written to awaken a generation to the power, potential, and preeminence of prayer in the kingdom. The book is provoking and practical in addressing our western culture and attitudes toward prayer. It identifies the prayer barriers of fear and idolatry and serves as a guide to help us overcome the obstacles that are not just holding us back as individuals but as communities, cities, and even nations. I highly recommend this book. It is easy to read, thoroughly sc your prayer life—in a good way!

CRAIG KRAFT
Executive director, Outreach Canada

This book has inspired me to reimagine th Christ's ascension ministry such as to expect a powerful and illuminating divine-human encounter. In practical terms, John's meticulous review of the "normative" place of prayer as established by the ministries of Christ and the apostles is having a strategic impact in the way I do mission and ministry.

PRESTON GRAHAM JR.
Senior pastor, Christ Presbyterian Church, New Haven, CT; director, Mission Anabaino

As a thirty-something millennial who grew up in the church, I've heard all the formulas for "super quick" post-Bible study prayer (popcorn prayer, anyone?). This book is not one of them. Gathering many of the Bible's references to prayer, John explores a pattern that reveals corporate prayer as not just a last-reserve tool for revival, but the sign of revival itself. This book is a powerful tool to spark revival.

ALEXA GILKER
Screenwriter

In my teens, I read E. M. Bounds and Andrew Murray on prayer and was greatly affected. And I have read numerous books on this topic since then. But *Prayer Revolution* is the one that has affected me most as an adult. It is deeply biblical and practical. John takes us through the Scriptures, which amounts to an adventure in prayer. I found myself praying my way through the book. As I did, you too will find yourself standing with the ascended Christ in the presence of the Father praying holistically. The result for me has been God-focused prayers with confidence and power. May His kingdom come!

RUSS SIMONS
WorldVenture missionary to Asia; consultant to WEA on prayer

Every generation of the church needs a prophetic voice to rouse it from complacency. Through *Prayer Revolution*, prepare to hear God calling you to a movement of prayer, revival, and renewal! It is clear, compelling, and constructive.

CONNAN KUBLIK
Director, Grace Network Canada; church planter, New City Church

I have read many informative and insightful books on prayer. Books that make me want to take notes and keep reading. But John's book is counterintuitive as written word. It does not inspire more reading. Rather, it makes me want to stop reading, set the book down . . . and pray . . . Thy kingdom come.

AL BREITCRUZ
Salvation Army team leader

This is a fresh view of prayer from a long-time faithful practitioner, placing it as an essential and strategic element in the progress of God's kingdom. One thinks of Paul who, at the end of presenting the various pieces of Christian armor, ends by tying them all, via a present participle, with the phrase: *praying at all times in the Spirit, with all prayer and supplication* (Eph. 6:18), as if to say: *This is the last and essential piece in the armor of God.* Thank you, John, for reminding us about the crucial place of prayer as we seek to promote the advancement of God's kingdom in times of much opposition.

REV. DR. PETER JONES
Director, truthXchange; adjunct professor, Westminster Seminary, CA

For several years now, I have had a growing sense that God is calling the church in North America to rediscover the place and power of corporate prayer. John Smed gives voice to this as he unpacks the Scriptures, church history, and our present-day need to recover a movement of corporate prayer. All who lead churches, ministries, and homes would do well to carefully read this book.

DARIN PESNELL
Lead pastor, ironworkschurch.org

Like the flashing stick-figure on my dash reminding me to buckle up before driving, *Prayer Revolution* reminds that prayer precedes any real advance of the gospel, and prayer is what sustains it. The biblical and historical evidence is there for us to see in John's book, and we need to heed the call to join in united prayer to partner with our Lord in His mission.

DAN RUTHERFORD
Founder, The Activate Course

The book you are holding in your hand is a treasure. With great clarity and deep conviction, John lays forth a vision for prayer that is expansive, invigorating, and most of all, deeply biblical. Few books have ever stirred my hunger for God and His coming kingdom like *Prayer Revolution*.

KEVIN JAMISON
Lead pastor, Sojourn East, Louisville

What a compelling biblical exposition rooted in missional conviction and practical insight.

MARK REYNOLDS
Vice President, Leadership Development, City to City

A must read if you want your church community or nation changed.

ROSE MARIE MILLER
Author of *Nothing Is Impossible with God*

The statement "corporate prayer is the soil in which vision from God grows from mustard seed to mighty plant, providing shade and shelter for many" is an invitation for our organization to remain faithful in prayer and believe God for great things.

LEE-ANNE MICHAYLUK
CEO, More than a Roof Housing Society

Packed with decades of pastoral insight, *Prayer Revolution* does not offer a formula of how to pray; rather, it gives the heart and philosophy of why we must pray.

KAREN ELLIS
Cannada Fellow for World Christianity, Reformed Theological Seminary

PRAYER REVOLUTION

*Rebuilding Church
and City Through Prayer*

JOHN SMED

MOODY PUBLISHERS

CHICAGO

Previously published as *Disruptive Prayer: The Movement Starts Here.*

Unless otherwise indicated, Scripture quotations are from the ESV® Bible (The Holy Bible, English Standard Version®), copyright © 2001 by Crossway, a publishing ministry of Good News Publishers. Used by permission. All rights reserved.

Scripture quotations marked NIV are taken from the Holy Bible, New International Version®, NIV®. Copyright © 1973, 1978, 1984, 2011 by Biblica, Inc.™ Used by permission of Zondervan. All rights reserved worldwide. www.zondervan.com. The "NIV" and "New International Version" are trademarks registered in the United States Patent and Trademark Office by Biblica, Inc.™

Scripture quotations marked NKJV are taken from the New King James Version. Copyright © 1982 by Thomas Nelson, Inc. Used by permission. All rights reserved.

Edited by Ginger Kolbaba
Interior design: Erik M. Peterson
Cover design: Thinkpen Design

All websites and phone numbers listed herein are accurate at the time of publication but may change in the future or cease to exist. The listing of website references and resources does not imply publisher endorsement of the site's entire contents. Groups and organizations are listed for informational purposes, and listing does not imply publisher endorsement of their activities.

Library of Congress Cataloging-in-Publication Data

Names: Smed, John, author.
Title: Prayer revolution : rebuilding Church and city through prayer / John Smed.
Description: Chicago : Moody Publishers, 2020. | Includes bibliographical references and index. | Summary: "Are you praying constricted prayers or disruptive ones? Most prayers are constricted ones. They're prayers that only focus on one part of the Lord's Prayer: "give us our daily bread." They're usually focused on self and envision God as a heavenly caretaker. Disruptive prayers, on the other hand, are powerful, uncommon, and deeply biblical. They focus on God rather than self, seek to advance the kingdom, and submit all things to God. They are also prayed with a profound belief that prayer actually accomplishes something. When we pray disruptive prayers, that's when the revolution begins. This book shows you how to equip leaders, fuel kingdom movements, and do real damage to the powers of darkness in the here and now. But most of all, discover how your own heart will be transformed as you begin to see how much bigger prayer, and God, is than you ever thought possible"-- Provided by publisher.
Identifiers: LCCN 2019055257 (print) | LCCN 2019055258 (ebook) | ISBN 9780802419873 (paperback) | ISBN 9780802498793 (ebook)
Subjects: LCSH: Prayer--Christianity. | Prayer--Biblical teaching.
Classification: LCC BV210.3 .S575 2020 (print) | LCC BV210.3 (ebook) | DDC 248.3/2--dc23
LC record available at https://lccn.loc.gov/2019055257
LC ebook record available at https://lccn.loc.gov/2019055258

Originally delivered by fleets of horse-drawn wagons, the affordable paperbacks from D. L. Moody's publishing house resourced the church and served everyday people. Now, after more than 125 years of publishing and ministry, Moody Publishers' mission remains the same—even if our delivery systems have changed a bit.

Moody Publishers
820 N. LaSalle Boulevard
Chicago, IL 60610

1 3 5 7 9 10 8 6 4 2

Printed in the United States of America

Dedication

To those inspiring brothers and sisters who have learned to pray through adversity and turn consternation into intercession for their persecutors—EW and Deborah in China, Aliesky in Cuba, and Jim, Daniel, Vijay, and Ebenezer in India. No one moves ahead without great friends and co-laborers like Bert and Carole Gibson, Evan and Marilynn Bottomley, and my constant colleague, Tom Wood.

Contents

THE WORLD AWAITS A PRAYER REVOLUTION

My purpose for writing this book is simple: to issue a biblical call to prayer that fuels a prayer movement for kingdom advance throughout North America.

The outcome we seek, though simple, is anything but small-minded. It is our constant prayer that our Savior King might pour out His Spirit to revive His church and renew our cities and land. The first evidence of the coming of Christ's kingdom will be a deep transformation of the character and activity of the church. These Holy Spirit changes cannot be contained. New light dispels the darkness; the yeast spreads throughout; the mustard seed takes root and grows. The result will be radical renewal of city life and restructuring of society in all its workings—indeed, it will be *revolutionary* in the most wonderful sense of the word.

We will experience "joy in the city" when people hear and receive the Good News (see Acts 8:8). As believers gather in earnest and united prayer, the gates of the city will "[open] for them of its own accord" (Acts 12:5, 10). As prayer relentlessly prevails against seen and unseen opposition, those who preach the gospel will once again be accused of turning "the world upside down" (Acts 17:6).

This is no humble aim to be confident we can attain an intensive movement of kingdom prayer considering the current anemic state of the church when it comes to prayer. It seems fanciful to claim that the present inertia can be reversed and that the doldrums be replaced by the Spirit's mighty wind of prayer.

Indeed, respected church and mission analysts have argued there is little likelihood of us experiencing a major advance of the kingdom in our context in the near future. Noted missiologist Ed Stetzer writes, "Church planting movements are unlikely to happen in our Western context within our generation."[1]

While this writer might provide an accurate description of our existing situation, the biblical narrative leaves little room for pessimistic predictions. In fact, in both Old and New Testaments we find that great revivals and attendant renewals are often quite literally "just a prayer away." It is in darkest times of decline, amid periods of stunning indifference to God's kingdom, that God often pours out a spirit of prayer and repentance, which becomes an overwhelming tide of truth that converts hearts and heals nations (see 2 Chron. 7:14; Zech. 12:10–13:2).

EVERYTHING REVOLUTION NEEDS IS IN THE SCRIPTURES

The scarcity of sources other than the Bible throughout *Prayer Revolution* is intentional. The biblical narrative concerning prayer and kingdom advance speaks for itself with unstoppable force and indisputable clarity. We have no great need for exegetical prowess or extra-biblical endorsement when the Bible admits no exceptions to the argument that prayer is at the forefront in every case of church revival and urban renewal. Nothing can improve upon the biblical argument for the primacy and priority of prayer. As Charles Haddon Spurgeon preached, "Let the pure gospel go forth in all its lion-like majesty, and it will soon clear its own way and ease itself of its adversaries."[2] *Prayer Revolution* is a biblical study, but it is not theoretical. I write as a practitioner and to encourage practitioners. In Christian community, I have studied and practiced kingdom prayer in the context of urban mission for more than thirty years. Ministries I served include extensive and intensive involvement with the church in North America: planting two churches, one in city-center Vancouver, British Columbia; serving as church-planting director of Mission to North America; and founding a Canada-wide church-planting team, The Grace Network. With a praying church and consecrated team, I have worked for three decades to insert kingdom prayer into movements and networks of church planting.

We devoted all our time and energy to fueling a movement of kingdom prayer. In 2012, God brought a passionate team together and we launched Prayer Current Ministries, an organization that "equips missional leaders to make disciples through prayer and build houses of prayer."[3] Since then our team has been involved in prayer discipleship throughout North America, Central America, and more recently in Asia and Europe.

More important than all these activities is our joy beholding God at work as He builds praying leaders and communities, as He sends them in boldness, joy, and power to reach their neighborhoods, cities, and countries for Christ. Many hundreds are becoming effective disciples through prayer. We are experiencing heaven's great joy as we see many come to Christ in our own backyard and wherever kingdom prayer multiplies. We're seeing, simply, a true prayer revolution.

Recently, we received this news from a missionary working in a closed country: "Just returned from the capital and time with P and A. They did a prayer-walking and evangelism event (his version of your training) with seven American students from a sister church and thirty people from his church. They gave 215 gospel presentations and ninety-five people received Christ. Gave away over two hundred Bibles. Glory!"

God is calling us to His work; therefore, *Prayer Revolution* is an experiential study. My colleagues and I at Prayer Current have firsthand testimony that coheres with the biblical narrative concerning prayer and kingdom advance. With no end of failures and admitted weaknesses, we can say we have walked the talk when it comes to prayer and kingdom advance. As with the above missionary's letter, we have seen the fruit and advance of prayer in evangelism and mission. As we pray, God answers. When we ask God for opportunity to share our faith, appointments multiply.

With grief and sadness, we have also seen the poverty and performance orientation when people attempt this mission without prayer at the center. The warnings of Isaiah 30:1 ring true and describe a good deal of what often passes for kingdom mission: "'Ah, stubborn children,' declares the LORD, 'who carry out a plan, but not mine, and who make an alliance, but not of my Spirit, that they may add sin to sin.'" Only God's almighty power is sufficient to revive the church and rebuild the city. All our preaching, teaching, programs, and outreaches are half-hearted until ignited by prayer.

DEFINING A KEY TERM

Throughout the book I refer to several related phrases—*kingdom prayer, the coming kingdom, the advance and expansion of the kingdom*—all of which beg for a clear definition of what we mean by the term *kingdom*. As one would expect, we have strong conceptions of what the term means. Rather than attempting to supply a single or simple definition of *kingdom,* which would be impossible in my estimation, I have added into every chapter an important facet to help our overall understanding of the biblical concept of the kingdom of God—and more specifically, the coming of the kingdom.

My intention is that the overall call to prayer in *Prayer Revolution* brings together several of the essential aspects of the coming of the kingdom in varied, inspiring ways. I only hope that we do justice to the great adventure of what it means to serve the King of kings and Lord of lords and become part of Jesus' mighty work in bringing the kingdom of God into the hearts and lives of all people!

You will find that I use the terms *kingdom movement* and *prayer movement* interchangeably. Quite simply, this is because there is no kingdom movement that is not fueled by prayer. At the same time, the concerted, united prayers of God's people initiate and permeate every advance of the kingdom. It is "gathered" prayer that is met with gale force winds and earthquakes.

I realize there are different, and even competing, conceptions of what the coming of the kingdom is about and therefore what constitutes kingdom prayer. My argument goes against the grain of some prevailing thought on the subject. I have chosen not to enter into the fray to dispute on these matters for a few reasons.

For one, this study is not intended to be the last word on prayer. Prayer is as rich and varied a topic as is our relationship with Christ, and it's as deep as the Scriptures themselves. Every praying believer is experiencing the Spirit of God and learning important lessons about prayer that can benefit the entire church.

Second, I have not written this book to discourage anyone who prays in faith to Christ. Rather, I hope to strengthen all who pray and to add some helpful and important insights along the way.

Third, while this book is not the last word on prayer, I am resolute that it *is* the first word. The biblical narrative supports the assertion that kingdom prayer has primacy and priority when it comes to kingdom advance—that every expansion of God's kingdom begins and is fueled by prayer.

Not far from where Prayer Current Ministries' work of kingdom prayer began in Vancouver lies the coastal region of Tofino—storm-ridden beaches consecrated to wave watching and surfing. On typical days, six-foot waves steadily advance toward the shore. In stormy seasons, however, the waves often reach up to forty feet, a stunning display of aquatic power that flings logs like twigs, lays waste to rickety piers, and dramatically reshapes the shoreline. For onlookers, it is terrifying yet thrilling to behold.

The kingdom of God, like the waves He commands, relentlessly advances. God Almighty shapes the world toward His intended destiny. At times the progress is steady and barely noticed, yet the yeast and salt of the kingdom are doing their work. This might describe kingdom advance in the Western world. At other times and places, the kingdom surges forward with violent force, and the earth-shaking forces of Pentecost are unleashed. Everything and everyone, seen and unseen, is buffeted by the advancing waves of spiritual upheaval. Both the church and the world are radically reshaped. This is revolution. *This* is revival.

When the sea is stormy, small faith prefers to observe from the shore. Greater faith longs to dive in and feel the pounding surf. Small prayers stay focused on the safe and predictable. Great prayers love to explore the torrent of God's power and reclaim the embrace of His love.

Prayer is how we seize the power of the Spirit and enter the powerful surge of the coming kingdom. Prayer is revolutionary, because the coming of the kingdom is revolutionary. Apart from prayer we remain spectators on the shore. But as we engage in prayer, we are caught up in the thrilling adventure of the kingdom of God and discover the unfolding plan of Christ.

Every kingdom movement starts with prayer. And so I invite you to enlist with a growing company of those who are learning to call out to our almighty Father, in the name of the enthroned Son, and who are experiencing the revolution of the Holy Spirit.

PART 1

—

KINGDOM PRAYER
BREAKS IN

THE KING COMES IN PRAYER

Jesus imparts His life of prayer through presence, teaching, and example. The coming of the King signals the coming of the kingdom.

The Bible's concept of kingdom is rich but not complicated. In its most simple sense, when Jesus tells us to pray, "Your kingdom come," He emphasizes that we are to live in light of His triumphant return. We live today in light of tomorrow. Christ's coming again frames the vision of every believer. As the new day steadily approaches, the ever-brighter splendor of His coming crests the horizon of cosmic history—lighting the way for kingdom advance. No present suffering, discouragement, or opposition can overcome our confident hope that Jesus will soon restore all things.

The coming of the kingdom is embedded in cosmic and world history. There is a time dynamic to the forward advance of the kingdom—from present day to final fulfillment. As the prophet foretold, "The great day of the LORD is near, near and hastening fast" (Zeph. 1:14).

From present day to final fulfillment, the window through which we survey the horizons of the coming kingdom is the coming of Christ. The kingdom of God is specifically the kingdom of Christ. It is Christ's comings that are the framework and cosmic backdrop to kingdom advance.

The beginning of kingdom history begins with Christ as the eternal Creator-King. As John 1:3 says, "All things were made through him, and without him was not any thing made that was made."

Jesus' kingdom comes in person when He "became flesh and dwelt among us" (John 1:14). In the incarnation of Jesus, the kingdom proper takes up residence in the domain of humankind. Reconciling heaven and earth through His blood, Jesus becomes the firstborn of the new humanity and the Redeemer of all creation. Jesus' resurrection from the dead is God's verdict that Christ's work is finished, final, and forever sufficient for completing every kingdom purpose: "[God has] declared [him] to be the Son of God in power according to the Spirit of holiness by his resurrection from the dead" (Rom. 1:4).

The kingdom moves from promise to realization when Jesus ascends and is exalted to the right hand of God. "From the cross to the grave, from the grave to the sky,"[1] Jesus ascends upward to the apex and summit of heaven and earth. The vulnerable Savior has become the invincible King of kings. Christ pours out His Holy Spirit from on high, the sum and symbol of His redemptive victory.

The eyes of faith are fixed ever upward to the enthroned King. The gaze of faith is ever forward to His imminent return.

Praying, especially praying together, is our means of experiencing the present ascension presence and power of Christ. As Jesus told His disciples, "Wait. . . . You will receive power when the Holy Spirit comes on you." And the disciples "joined together constantly in prayer" (Acts 1:4, 8, 14 NIV). Prayer is the instrument and means by which believers are sustained until Jesus returns. All prayer is now kingdom prayer, as all prayer is mediated through Christ, every promise guaranteed by His power and magnificence.

THE KING COMES IN PRAYER

As we contemplate Jesus' life among us, a central observation emerges—that the King comes in prayer. Jesus lived a life of prayer. He navigated His life by prayer. He enjoyed uninterrupted fellowship with the Father. Through His prayers, Jesus called down from heaven infinite grace and power to inaugurate and advance the kingdom. By His life of prayer, His teachings on prayer, and His giving us a spirit of prayer, Jesus births a praying people. As praying people, the following is what we need to understand.

For a Life of Prayer, We Find All We Need in Jesus

While there are many kinds of prayer, Christian prayer is all about Jesus. It is Christ-centric. Jesus not only brings believers through the veil dividing them from God, He removes the barrier altogether. Through Christ every Christian takes residence in the very throne room of God, with Jesus providing everything we need to ensure our constant communion with God. As the writer of Hebrews wrote, "Since then we have a great high priest . . . let us then with confidence draw near to the throne of grace" (4:14, 16). We not only have Jesus' example and teaching, we also have His personal friendship, His mediation, and His presence in prayer.

Jesus Offers Every Believer a Prayer Friendship

Those who pray experience intimacy with Christ as He reveals His plans and purposes: "The servant does not know what his master is doing; but I have called you friends, for all that I have heard from my Father I have made known to you . . . so that whatever you ask the Father in my name, he may give it to you" (John 15:15–16).

True prayer is friendship prayer—friendship with Jesus. Who doesn't need a good friend? A friend is someone you can always confide in. A friend is someone you can always rely on. Realizing that Jesus is your best and truest friend in prayer opens a whole new world of confidence and adventure.

Jesus Mediates Our Prayers

As we pray, Jesus as our mediator prays with and for us on the basis of His finished work on the cross. This is an astounding truth and great blessing in prayer: we can cast aside guilt and doubt when we offer our prayers in the name of Jesus, for "who is to condemn? Christ Jesus is the one who died—more than that, who was raised—who is at the right hand of God, who indeed is interceding for us" (Rom. 8:34).

Jesus Purifies Our Prayers

Our prayers are made acceptable in the mediatory work of Jesus. This image is found in Leviticus 16:12–13 and Revelation 8.

In Leviticus we read that once a year, on the great Day of Atonement, the high priest offered a sacrifice on the burning altar. After taking bloodied and burning coals from the altar, he placed them in a censer and filled the censer with two handfuls of incense. As the high priest entered the Most Holy Place, symbolizing the very presence of God, he waved the censer so that a fragrant smoke billowed and filled the room. As the cloud of incense covered the mercy seat, God was pleased with the fragrance and accepted the sacrifices and offerings for His people.

Corresponding to this Old Testament drama, in Revelation, John described the parallel experience as a believer prays today.

When any believer enters the throne room, the incense of their prayer ascends to God. The believer's pleas and praises are mixed with the blood of the Savior, resulting in fragrant, purified, and pleasing petitions to God:

> Another angel came and stood at the altar with a golden censer, and he was given much incense to offer with the prayers of all the saints on the golden altar before the throne, and the smoke of the incense, with the prayers of the saints, rose before God from the hand of the angel.
>
> REVELATION 8:3–4

God answers such Christ-filled prayers with powerful transformations that not only change the one who prays, but also that shake the world and shape its destiny. As John continued, "The angel took the censer and filled it with fire from the altar and threw it on the earth, and there were peals of thunder, rumblings, flashes of lightning, and an earthquake" (Rev. 8:5).

Every believer has confidence entering the most holy presence of God through the blood sacrifice of Jesus. Jesus carries us into heaven itself. This high-priestly work of Christ brings a profound and enduring boldness to our prayers (see Heb. 10:19–22).

This is what it means to pray in Jesus' name; as we pray, we invoke the purifying merit of His mediatory work.

Jesus Indwells Us in His Spirit of Prayer

In order that we might enjoy answer upon answer to our prayers, Jesus gives each believer His Spirit of prayer. Often we do not know how to pray; the Holy Spirit dwells deep within every believer and "groans" alongside us. Often we do not know what to ask for; the Holy Spirit teaches us to pray the right thoughts and words (see Rom. 8:26–27).

Whenever we find ourselves stumped in prayer, Jesus encourages us that the Father always gives the Holy Spirit to those who ask (see Luke 11:9–13).

JESUS' PRACTICE OF PRAYER IS THE PERFECT EXAMPLE FOR US

Jesus' life of prayer is outlined in fullness and detail, especially in the book of Luke, to furnish a clear pattern for how we, like Jesus, are to navigate life by prayer, enjoy our union with God through prayer, and call down the kingdom realities of grace and power using prayer.

I recall the first time I earnestly studied the many passages about Jesus' prayer life from Luke's Gospel. It was a number of years after I had done a major study in the book of Acts about the priority of prayer. I had not yet connected the prayer life of the early church to the prayer life of Jesus. Luke wrote both a Gospel by his name and the book of Acts, so it is not surprising that Luke stressed the theme of prayer in both. Over several weeks, I studied the prayer life of Jesus. I discovered that prayer was a first priority of the apostolic church simply because prayer was a first priority of Jesus. The deeper I went in Luke's Gospel, I found it was not only Jesus' teaching about prayer but His very praying life that could impart a spirit of prayer.

The outcome for me was inescapable. Jesus lived a life of prayer and Jesus said, "Follow me!" If I was going to follow Him and become like Him, I needed to live a life of prayer as He did. I knew this would be revolutionary and would disrupt my way of life, but I knew it would be infinitely worth it.

Immersing myself in the prayer practices of Jesus, my prayer life changed. Praying like Jesus became a discipline and a habit.

Like Jesus praying all night before choosing His disciples, before major decisions and crossroads, I take seasons and days of prayer. Our team does not make plans, we make prayer plans—meeting regularly for interactive times of prayer and planning. We have learned to face the ever-present onslaught of electronic noise and busyness by waiting on God. I often share days of prayer and fasting with others going through severe trial. Like Jesus, who met exhaustion by withdrawing to pray, I am growing in the practice of conversing with God and laying down the many burdens that cling to my soul. Like Jesus, I want to have a contagious prayer life. I follow Jesus and I strive to lead others by example. Prayer is more caught than taught.

Jesus is the supreme teacher of prayer, and He invites us into His school of prayer. He demonstrates to us what a praying life looks like. He provides a model for prayer with very specific prayer practices, and we can overlay His prayer life on ours to cultivate richer prayer lives.

I invite you to learn what a praying life is about by studying the prayer life of Jesus. One at a time these texts from Luke's gospel have weight, yet read together, they will carry you to new heights of joy and adventure in prayer.

As you read, pray. Allow the Word to do the speaking. Ask the Holy Spirit to teach you what you need to learn from Jesus' life of prayer. His practice of prayer is presented in detail. As you follow His example step by step, you will learn to emulate Him in prayer. You too will be convicted to withdraw from a crowded life and find more time alone with God. Like Jesus, you will take extended time to pray before you make plans. Jesus talked with God all the time and will teach you the art of conversational prayer. The great reward for following this example is that your prayers will move from one-way words to a distant God to confiding with

> **Prayer is the first breath of a new believer. Once the first breath happens, the rest of life is simply a matter of continuing to breathe.**

a Friend. And as you follow Jesus' life as your guide, you will experience more of the following:

From the Start, Jesus Lived a Life of Prayer

Jesus' baptism inaugurated His ministry. The Spirit fell upon Him while He was praying:

> When all the people were baptized, and when Jesus also had been baptized and was praying, the heavens were opened, and the Holy Spirit descended on him in bodily form, like a dove; and a voice came from heaven, "You are my beloved Son; with you I am well pleased."
>
> LUKE 3:21–22

Similarly, the entire Christian life begins with prayer. Prayer is the first breath of a new believer. If that first breath does not happen, life cannot begin. Once the first breath happens, the rest of life is simply a matter of continuing to breathe.

Before Jesus began His public ministry, He prayed, fasted, and fought the devil for forty days: "Jesus, full of the Holy Spirit, returned from the Jordan and was led by the Spirit in the wilderness for forty days, being tempted by the devil" (Luke 4:1–2).

Those who are weak in faith meet adversity with anxiety. Jesus' followers face the enemy with prayer and with power.

Jesus Prayed to Recover from Ministry Chaos

We leave our busy lives to pray. Jesus left His praying life to be busy: "Even more the report about him went abroad, and great crowds gathered to hear him and to be healed of their infirmities. But he would withdraw to desolate places and pray" (Luke 5:15–16).

Jesus Prayed in Advance of Major Decisions

At every critical juncture, Jesus turned to prayer: "He went out to the mountain to pray, and all night he continued in prayer to God. And when day came, he called his disciples and chose from them twelve, whom he named apostles" (Luke 6:12–13).

For Jesus, prayer initiated every kingdom advance. The author Luke took pains to present this fact with indisputable detail. How much more should this become true of us? How foolish for us to make our important plans and decisions with little or no prayer! Planning for the future moves us from anxiety and uncertainty to adventure and opportunity when we immerse our decision-making in prayer. As we pray and fast, we partner with Christ, and we learn to yield to the guidance of the Holy Spirit.

Jesus at Prayer Elicited the First Great Confession

Time and again, Jesus retreated to be alone with God, and the disciples noticed. Eventually, they realized this man of prayer was the Son of God:

> It happened that as he was praying alone, the disciples were with him. And he asked them, "Who do the crowds say that I am?" And they answered, "John the Baptist. But others say, Elijah, and others, that one of the prophets of old has risen." Then he said to them, "But who do you say that I am?" And Peter answered, "The Christ of God."
>
> LUKE 9:18–20

Someone once said, "We are what we pray." Jesus' identity is most clearly revealed as He prays. Likewise, our true identity is revealed by our prayer lives. Others cannot fail to notice.

While Praying, Jesus Was Transfigured

Prayer is the environment for transfiguration: "About eight days after these sayings he took with him Peter and John and James and went up on the mountain to pray. And as he was praying, the appearance of his face was altered, and his clothing became dazzling white" (Luke 9:28–29).

It is while He prayed that Jesus manifested His glory. It is in earnest prayer that Christ's followers see the vision of His splendor and glory. As we pray, our vision of Christ is like looking at the sun in its full strength. Paul put it this way, "We all, with unveiled face, beholding the glory of the Lord, are being transformed into the same image from one degree of glory to another" (2 Cor. 3:18).

Jesus' Prayer Life Inspired His Disciples to Pray

Jesus not only prayed—His prayer life was contagious: "Jesus was praying in a certain place, and when he finished, one of his disciples said to him, 'Lord, teach us to pray, as John taught his disciples'" (Luke 11:1).

The disciples had just returned from a mission trip. They preached the gospel, healed the sick, and fought demonic forces. They were excited by their ministry but had awakened to the enormous challenges before them. Prayer moved them from pious practice to urgent necessity. Hungry for Jesus' power and peace, the disciples turned to the Great Teacher to learn His secret of kingdom advance.

When believers leave the safe confines of the local church, they discover the deep joys and great challenges of the harvest field. This brings a growing hunger for prayer. Those who step forth in obedience to the mission urgently seek out Christ to teach them how to pray.

Jesus Cleansed the Temple Because of Prayer

Jesus was hailed as Messiah as He entered the city. Descending from the Mount of Olives, He surveyed Jerusalem and wept for her. She had no eyes or heart for His coming, and Jesus prophesied terrible judgments on the city and her inhabitants: "Your enemies will set up a barricade around you and surround you and hem you in on every side and tear you down to the ground, you and your children within you . . . because you did not know the time of your visitation" (Luke 19:43–44).

The next day, Jesus entered the temple and, eaten up by jealousy for God's honor, His words of judgment became actions of wrath: "He entered the temple and began to drive out those who sold, saying to them, 'It is written, "My house shall be a house of prayer," but you have made it a den of robbers'" (Luke 19:45–46).

At the temple we see Jesus as we have never seen Him before. He held court, pronounced the verdict, and executed the judgment of God. The reason for His fury was straightforward but profound: God intended His temple to be a place for all nations to gather in prayer. All the splendor of this building, the temple service, teaching, and sacrifices meant nothing if prayer for the nations was missing.

The same holds true today. The cleansing of the temple is a monumental call to prayer for all time. Building projects, Sunday services, excellent programs, and offerings of money and time mean nothing if we are not building the Father's house of prayer for a lost world.

In Anguished Prayer, Jesus Prepared for the Cross

Jesus could not have faced the cross without prayer. He did not set aside His human nature to bear our sin; He faced the cross in His full humanity in order to be our sacrificial representative. As

He cried out in prayer, His approaching suffering was more than He could possibly bear: "Being in agony he prayed more earnestly; and his sweat became like great drops of blood falling down to the ground" (Luke 22:44).

Jesus was only able to face His greatest challenge by collapsing before His Father in prayer. How much more do we need to face the most significant challenges of life and death by crying out to our Father?

Jesus Forgave His Enemies on the Cross

The challenge of forgiveness is in proportion to the cost of forgiveness. It is no challenge to forgive a nickel debt; it is a considerable challenge to forgive a million-dollar debt. The highest cost of forgiveness is to forgive someone for taking a life. Jesus settled the debts of forgiveness because He paid the highest price: "Jesus said, 'Father, forgive them, for they know not what they do.' And they cast lots to divide his garments" (Luke 23:34).

The greater the injury done to us, the greater the need for us to ask again and again for Christ's spirit of forgiving prayer. An unknown poet put it this way:

> "Forgiving again?" I asked in dismay. "Must I keep forgiving
> and forgiving always?"
> "No," said the angel, whose eye pierced me through. "Stop
> forgiving when the Savior stops forgiving you."

Jesus Surrendered His Soul in Prayer

Jesus began His ministry in prayer, and He ended His ministry in prayer:

> It was now about the sixth hour, and there was darkness over the whole land until the ninth hour, while the sun's light failed. And the curtain of the temple was torn in

two. Then Jesus, calling out with a loud voice, said, "Father, into your hands I commit my spirit!" And having said this he breathed his last.

LUKE 23:44–46

This cosmic prayer of surrender expressed Christ's final release and paramount accomplishment for humankind. Prayer and surrender are synonymous—all true and effective prayer commits our spirit into the hands of God.

Jesus Prayed Blessing upon His Followers at His Ascension

As He ascended to His eternal reign, Jesus lifted His hands to pray: "He led them out as far as Bethany, and lifting up his hands he blessed them. While he blessed them, he parted from them and was carried up into heaven" (Luke 24:50–51).

His hands are lifted still! He ever lives to pray His resurrection blessings upon His people (see Rom. 8:34). Just so, we are never more like the risen and exalted Christ than when we bless others in intercession.

IMITATION IS MUCH MORE THAN FLATTERY

The Christian life is many things, but it certainly involves the active imitation of Christ. Imitating others is not wrong. Paul told the Corinthian believers, "Be imitators of me, as I am of Christ" (1 Cor. 11:1).

We can imitate Jesus by following the example of godly women and men of prayer—people who model a life of prayer. Their contagious integrity draws us into their leadership. We intuit that their godliness comes from following Jesus. Their passion for God makes us want to imitate them so that we, too, can experience and enter the prayer life of Jesus.

Older and wiser believers who model integrity of life, largeness of faith, and passion for mission reveal what following Jesus looks like to those coming after them. Sheep follow their shepherds. The next generation depends on it!

Kingdom-Come Prayer Today

1. Evaluate your prayer life in light of Jesus' prayer life. Note where you find differences. Ask God to help you lead and serve "from the knees," as Jesus did.

2. In what ways are you currently handling major decisions or challenges? To what degree are you driven by worry rather than empowered through prayer? What will it take to move from anxiety to adventure?

3. Isaiah 30:15 tells us, "In returning and rest you shall be saved; in quietness and in trust shall be your strength." When depleted and exhausted, what do you do? How do you feel about taking a day of restful prayer as Jesus did?

2

THE KING'S STRATEGY FOR PRAYER

Jesus' prayer expands our heart for God and His mission

Jesus came to build a new world, and this calls for a new prayer. Not just any prayer will do. He trains His disciples in a prayer that contains the architecture and strategy to advance the kingdom. He gives them a prayer that will increase their capacity for God and expand their heart for others.

Jesus knows we need help to pray—we do not know what to ask for and we do not know how to ask. In order to impart His purposes and His passion for prayer, He gives an all-encompassing framework to guide our prayers. Praying the priorities of this prayer is the key to the growth and advance of the kingdom of God. It is the prayer of all prayers. We call it "The Lord's Prayer."

When the disciples approached Jesus and requested, "Lord, teach us to pray," they had seen Jesus "praying in a certain place." They realized that His peace with God and His power for mission flowed from a life of prayer. They were hungry to experience the same peace and power. They were eager to know the secret of effective prayer. Jesus responded to the disciples' request by providing them—and us—with a comprehensive framework, a grid for prayer.

A PRAYER FOR BUSY PEOPLE

We have always been busy. Even Jesus was so busy He had to retreat to pray. Today's world is not only busy, it lacks cohesion—fragmented and distracted as it is by digital media and technology. We are devoted to scientific progress but have no faith trajectory. We move at breakneck speed but have no purpose or destiny to chart the course. It is marvelous how the prayer of Jesus speaks to this very need for cohesive focus and purpose. Using the Lord's Prayer as a framework for prayer is one way of incorporating structure into a busy and fragmented life. (See appendix B for more information on how to use the Lord's Prayer in your daily life.)

Life can be overwhelming in its busyness and complexity. Unless we bring form and purpose to our prayers, an unstructured life will lead to scattered and harried prayers—the kind that lack power and don't do much for starting or continuing a revolution.

But when we take the time to study and apply it to our daily lives—in particular breaking it down into seven specific parts, or what I call the "grid"—it works to bring a dynamic form and compelling purpose to guide and shape our prayer lives.

Renee Reynolds, a prayer director for Geneva School in New York City, has been using the Lord's Prayer as a framework for her prayers for years. She told me:

> *Using the seven-day prayer outline has fortified my prayer life with structure, dimension, and meaning—but most of all, it has brought a God-aligned focus and God-glorifying intent.*

I find the grid a simple tool that can be adapted to suit a diversity of people and personalities. Noting answered prayers fosters ongoing gratitude and reinvigorated prayer.

As you faithfully and thoughtfully pray "the grid," your prayer life, indeed your whole life, will evidence an order and purpose radically distinct from those surrounding you. Even more, as God empowers and answers your prayers, the light of His powerful grace will shine through you. Others will want to know the secret of hope within you.

A PRAYER TO BUILD THE KINGDOM

As soon as we get down on our knees, we want God to hear and answer our prayers. You may ask, What is effective prayer? How can I pray in such a way as to please God? Where should I focus my prayers? What is the scope of prayer?

These are terrific questions, and Jesus has an answer. He has given us a simple but comprehensive outline for prayer that is filled with promise and purpose. This prayer is a summary of what God's kingdom is all about and how we can be united to God and participate in His saving purposes in the world. Each petition is packed with implications for each believer, church, and the world we live in.

"Our Father in heaven,
hallowed be your name.
Your kingdom come,
your will be done,
on earth as it is in heaven.
Give us this day our daily bread,
and forgive us our debts,

> as we also have forgiven our debtors.
> And lead us not into temptation,
> but deliver us from evil."

MATTHEW 6:9–13

As you pray this prayer, the words may sound like so many high-sounding phrases. However, as you will see, each petition is rich with various purposes and can be adapted to anyone's life and situation. This prayer is alive in a spiritual and organic sense. It is not a matter of just repeating the words, like a prayer ritual. It is a matter of praying Jesus' meaning and intent. Pray this prayer thoughtfully, and you will find that the Lord's Prayer is flexible. Pray its meaning, and it will wonderfully expand to fit your world.

Because this is a prayer Jesus gave, it cannot fail to be heard and answered. Each request of Jesus' prayer contains the promise that God will hear you and will give you specific answers to your prayers. At the same time, the Holy Spirit will be doing a good work within you. From deep within, you will discover your connection to God is growing as well as is your love for others. Two great transformations occur: praying this prayer increases your heart capacity for God and expands your heart for others.

First, the capacity of your heart for God will dramatically increase. The priority of the Lord's Prayer is the Lord, therefore meaningful and effective prayer begins with a focus on God. His fatherhood, holy name, kingdom, and will are the heart and wellspring of this prayer. Worshiping God, seeking His kingdom, and acting on His will raise your prayers from mundane matters to eternal realities.

The central answer to our prayer is God. God is eager to give Himself to us. Jesus assures those who pray that God will give them the Holy Spirit: "How much more will the heavenly Father give the Holy Spirit to those who ask him!" (Luke 11:13). Prayer is the affectionate reaching out of our hearts for God. In one of his sermons, Augustine said it well, "It is prayer that develops our desire, and enlarges our heart until it is capable of containing God's gift of himself."[1]

Second, your heart for others will expand when you share Christ's own passion for His church and His sacrificial love for a lost world. Pray this prayer and you will move from uncaring selfishness to wholehearted intercession. God will lift you from the narrow confines of present urgencies to the majestic vision of a world transformed through answered prayer. Your commitment and resolve to build Christ's kingdom will deepen. Slowly but certainly, you will embody the Lord's kingdom values and be compelled to carry out His kingdom directives. As He fills you with His Spirit, you will become salt of the earth, light of the world, and yeast that spreads throughout a lost and needy world.

> **The problem with default prayer is not so much what we ask for but how our prayer is wrongly focused.**

THE CORRECT DIRECTION OF OUR PRAYERS

We become what we pray. When prayer neglects Christ's kingdom priorities, it becomes constricted and suffocates under a burden of present urgencies. We call this default prayer, in which our prayers focus on a random set of personal problems and health-related challenges. This kind of prayer accomplishes little transformation for those who pray and little for the world in which we live. Answers are few and far between.

While we can gladly and expectantly bring our daily cares and needs to God, this should not be the focus or extent of our prayers. The problem with default prayer is not so much what we ask for but how our prayer is wrongly focused. The object of this kind of prayer is self, not God. It is basically selfish: self is turned in on self and life is seen through self. We pray default prayer because we are looking at life through the wrong end of the telescope. The only object of true prayer is God, when life is viewed from God's perspective.

DEFAULT PRAYER
constricts our capacity for God and others

While in Coimbatore, India, I spent two days with the leaders and staff of Serve India, and I experienced with renewed clarity the expansive capacities of the Lord's Prayer. I was showing the group how to use the Lord's Prayer as a grid to bring a kingdom framework and purpose to their prayers. As we discussed and prayed, I came to my own liberating realization: not only did praying according to Jesus' "grid" bring a high purpose and kingdom order to my prayer life, but it also expanded my heart into the greater parameters of the kingdom. Praying the way Jesus taught us was increasing my capacity for God and expanding my heart for others.

Even as I was teaching others, God was speaking to me about my prayers. He revealed a negative tendency: I had been neglecting the habit to pray using the pattern of the Lord's Prayer and the result was that my prayer requests were becoming constricted to personal urgencies and concerns. I was not asking for wrong things, but my prayers were too self-focused. God opened my eyes to see that praying according to the Lord's Prayer was a powerful way to counter this tendency.

When I neglected to pray as Jesus taught, I lost a great deal of the joy and power I experienced when using the Lord's Prayer. The contrast was obvious.

I went back to the grid of the Lord's Prayer. Beginning with the first four petitions of the prayer, I start by meditating on the fatherhood of God, move to reverencing His holy name, progress to enjoying the splendor and majesty of His kingdom, and then surrender my heart, yielding to His will. The longer I continue a thoughtful and interactive practice of focusing on God, slowly but surely, my capacity for God is growing.

As I pray the last three petitions by praying for others' needs and then my own, my perspective changes. The more I pray for "today's bread," the more I experience personal contentment and generosity. By repeatedly asking God to forgive my debts, I am enabled both to extend and receive forgiveness. Praying this way is making me a kinder person. As I ask to be delivered from temptation and to be guided by God's Spirit, I am placing myself and others under God's protection. In the process, my experience of God's leading moves from theory to reality.

Praying the way Jesus prayed sets me free from constricted prayer, opens my heart to receive God's gift of Himself, and reverses my selfish tendencies.

As it turns out, God was communicating a similar message to

the Indian leaders. At lunch a young man, alight with passionate energy, asked if I would capture his prayer testimonial on video to share with people in North America. He said:

> This has been a divine revelation. My fingers were tingling as you spoke. I could feel I was being filled with the Spirit when you taught us how to pray the Lord's Prayer. Many people in India believe that if they simply say the words of this prayer, they are Christians. This is a very great error. You have been teaching us that if we pray this way, we will be praying for great and important things.

In contrast to default prayer, the Lord's Prayer is the prayer Jesus gives His people. This is the prayer Jesus prayed, and the Father always hears the Son (see John 11:41). As God answers these seven petitions, the aims, values, and goals of Christ's kingdom enter the fabric and heart of our lives. As the diagram below illustrates, the Lord's Prayer increases our capacity for God and expands our heart for others.

Left to ourselves, the gravity of our fallen nature draws us into self; like the wood shaving of a carpenter's plane, life tightly curls into a little circle. In contrast, Jesus' prayer sends our hearts upward and expands our hearts outward. No matter which part of the Lord's Prayer I focus on, I recognize the need to empty myself of selfishness and to ask to be filled with His greater life and Spirit.

As our prayers constrict, they tend to be sparse on praise and focused on limited requests. For example, at various Bible studies and meetings, invariably the time comes for prayer requests. For some unknown reason, most requests start with a narrative of someone's health crisis and the request is for physical healing. We seldom begin our prayers with extended times of meaningful

worship. We become problem-centered, which suffocates effective prayer. Without guidance and good teaching, our prayers seldom escape the gravity of our small world, even though we have many other important things we should be praying for.

Jesus gave us a prayer to reverse the gravity of selfishness and to move from a constricted prayer life to an effective prayer life. We have no better way to make a joyous and fruitful disciple than to teach them the deep meaning and practical use of the Lord's Prayer.

The issue is critical. When God is growing His church and bringing salvation to the world, He always raises up strong men and women of prayer. If we hope to raise up a new generation of harvest workers, we need to set before them the life-changing mandates of kingdom prayer. Kingdom advance begins when we make disciples through prayer. As we multiply leaders, prayer and prayer meetings will take expression in church, home, public sector, marketplace, places of education, and government.

For example, in recent years, I, along with my church and our prayer ministry, have served a larger faith-based public-housing organization in Vancouver called More Than a Roof. In ten housing projects, this ministry serves new immigrants, single parents, people in drug and alcohol recovery, and those struggling with mental illness. The staff and volunteer team are careful about sharing their faith—they do only if they are asked—but they are free to pray for one another and for their tenants. They asked our prayer team to help them overcome discouragement about unanswered prayers. Their earnest petitions for significant needs were not always answered, and some were becoming discouraged. The director asked us to address the issue of answers to prayer.

We asked the participants to consider a few simple questions:

(1) "What are you asking God for?" We understand that the answer we get will depend on the requests we make.
(2) "What will answers look like if you pray the requests of the Lord's Prayer?"

As we helped these leaders discuss and pray through the Lord's Prayer, a whole new world opened. Moving beyond the crises of health, finances, mental illness, and addiction, they were learning to put God first, to aim vertically, to rest in His love, to worship Him in holy joy, and to seek His kingdom and will. Deepening in our joy of God's presence and rejoicing in His work was the answer of all answers. When we ask for God first, our prayer is always answered. He delights to give us Himself in the gift of the Holy Spirit (see Luke 11:13).

Continuing the sequence of the Lord's Prayer, we moved from

vertical prayers to praying for one another. This led to practical requests for daily bread, reconciliation, forgiveness in their community, bold prayers for justice, and requests for deliverance from evil. This expanded the horizons of their requests to kingdom proportions. Discouragement about unanswered prayer was simply being expelled by this new focus.

When a prayer group discovers the immensity and majesty of God's kingdom purposes, we find that people begin to raise the roof in earnest, united prayer. Prayer moves from "I have to pray" to "I get to pray."

THE SEVEN PRIORITIES OF THE LORD'S PRAYER AND HOW GOD ANSWERS

It is common for people to complain that their prayers are not being answered. "I prayed and nothing happened," they say. My reply is, "God's answer depends on what you ask for." One encouraging way to look at the Lord's Prayer is to break it down one petition—one priority—at a time, and ask what it looks like when God grants our requests.

"Our Father in Heaven"

As we pray "Our Father in heaven," God answers by imparting a childlike love and trust to our souls. When we address God as Father, every prayer transforms from ritual to relationship.

As we pray "Our Father in heaven," we acknowledge a common humanity, made in God's image, with one God as everyone's Creator. God's answer is to break down the hidden tribalism, nationalism, or racism hidden in our souls.

God is the Redeemer-Father of all believers. As we pray "Our Father in heaven," by His Spirit we grow in love for other believers and become passionate for the unity of the church. We call every believer in Christ brother or sister, and we gladly pray for them.

"Hallowed be Your Name"

When we pray "Hallowed be Your name," we gain a humble sense of awe at God's holiness. We are renewed in reverence and become jealous for His name to be honored and His fame to spread throughout the world. We pray for the pure worship of God in His church. With this fuller vision of God, we experience new depths of repentance and new fillings of joy.

When we pray "Hallowed be Your name," we grieve when people misuse or dishonor His name or fail to give Him thanks. We focus our resolve on proclaiming the fame and glory of God to those who do not know Him (see Ps. 96). We anticipate a day when all humankind will be a multinational, multibillion voice choir!

"Your Kingdom Come"

As we call out from the heart "Your kingdom come," we rejoice in Christ's rule and reign over all things, especially His church, and we are captured by the majesty of His mission. As we go deep in prayer, Jesus gives us His heart for those who do not know Him, so that we understand His concern: "When he saw the crowds, he had compassion for them, because they were harassed and help-less, like sheep without a shepherd" (Matt. 9:36). Our prayers are filled with zeal for His mission: "The harvest is plentiful, but the laborers are few; therefore pray earnestly to the Lord of the har-vest" (Matt. 9:37–38).

As we pray, we move from being spectators to becoming par-ticipants in His mission: "The Son of Man came to seek and to save the lost" (Luke 19:10). As Jesus prayed, "As you sent me into the world, so I have sent them into the world" (John 17:18). As we pray, His purpose becomes ours: that many people will come to Christ and that revival in the church and renewal for the city will follow (see Zech. 13:1–2).

"Your Will Be Done on Earth as It Is in Heaven"

When we pray "Your will be done on earth as it is in heaven," a miracle happens within. God's will moves into our hearts. From within, we strive to accept His will, no matter how difficult things get. We learn to approve God's will as good, right, and just; we resolve to act on His will in loving obedience.

As we faithfully pray "Your will be done on earth as it is in heaven," we feel our souls burn with God's love of righteousness and justice: "What does the LORD require of you but to do justice, and to love kindness, and to walk humbly with your God?" (Mic. 6:8). We move from being overwhelmed by the injustice of the world to becoming agents of its renewal. Our kingdom prayers bring justice and mercy to realization. We become God's answer to our own prayers. As the prophet Isaiah tells us:

> You shall call, and the LORD will answer;
>> you shall cry, and he will say, "Here I am" . . .
> if you pour yourself out for the hungry
>> and satisfy the desire of the afflicted . . .
>> you shall raise up the foundations of many generations;
> you shall be called the repairer of the breach,
>> the restorer of streets to dwell in.
>
> ISAIAH 58:9–10, 12

"Give Us This Day Our Daily Bread"

As we request of God to "give us this day our daily bread," we grow in firm assurance that we will have enough resources for ourselves and plenty to care for the poor and needy. Our hearts become generous, and our needs modest. We are filled with a new spirit of thanksgiving.

As we pray "Give us this day our daily bread," we learn contentment and generosity. We don't just talk about helping others in need, we start doing it, giving our time and releasing our resources and opening our homes to the poor, displaced, disabled, immigrant, or otherwise outcast.

"Forgive Us Our Debts as We Forgive Our Debtors"

When we humbly pray "Forgive us our debts as we forgive our debtors," we ask God to impart His Spirit and grant redemptive community. God gives us a deep inner peace as we accept and enjoy His forgiveness. Whether in the church or in the world, we begin to treat others with humility and grace.

> **We do not pray about spiritual warfare. Prayer itself is spiritual warfare.**

As we bow in humble repentance, asking God to "forgive us our debts as we forgive our debtors," He makes us agents of reconciliation. An elderly friend knew her cancer was a death sentence. She told me, "I was praying, 'Forgive us our debts,' and all of a sudden, I knew my heart was filled with grudges toward family members. I realized how foolish I was. I phoned each of them to say 'I am sorry.' They forgave me. Now they are all coming here for a family reunion." As she conveyed this story, her eyes radiated pure joy.

"Lead Us Not into Temptation, but Deliver Us from the Evil One"

When we pray "Lead us not into temptation, but deliver us from the evil one," God fortifies our souls against the incessant temptations of the world and the devil. Guided by the Good Shepherd, we grow confident that He will lead us in the way we should go—in His "paths of righteousness for his name's sake" (Ps. 23:3).

When we pray this petition, we are like Frodo Baggins in J. R. R. Tolkien's *The Lord of the Rings*. As soon as he put on the ring of power, the unseen world became visible to him. Frodo was able to see the enemy—and the enemy was able to see him. The contest between good and evil commenced the minute he put on the ring.

In a similar way, as soon as we start praying, we enter the fray. We do not pray about spiritual warfare. Prayer itself is spiritual warfare. We are not overwhelmed or fearful, because Jesus came to destroy the works of the devil (see 1 John 3:8), and indeed He did. At the cross, He dealt the deathblow to the evil one.

Praying "Lead us not into temptation" makes us aware of the evil, proud, licentious, and anti-Christian nature of the world around us—and the world within us too. We join others praying against the predatory and immoral actions of those who deceive others, who use all manner of schemes to exploit people, from dishonest marketing to human trafficking. We cultivate godliness and encourage strong boundaries around our churches, families, and communities. We endeavor to use "just weights" and honest communications in all our dealings.

When we ask our heavenly Father for something, we should lift our eyes and hearts in expectation of an answer. Jesus taught, "Ask, and it will be given to you" (Matt. 7:7). The Lord's Prayer is not the only prayer we should pray; Scripture presents thousands of prayers we can pray. But Jesus has given us words to provide a helpful guide to how we should pray and what we should ask for. Each petition of this prayer promises an answer.

WHAT JESUS' PRAYER ACCOMPLISHES

Jesus created a new world order—and He gave a prayer to accomplish that end. Meditating on and then praying these seven petitions on your own and in community will forever deliver you from constricted and self-focused prayer. It will introduce you to—and invite you into—the advance of God's kingdom.

Our Lord aims to transform us into His likeness. He honors us by enlisting us in His world-changing mission. In order to expand our hearts and accomplish His kingdom purposes, He teaches us to pray the directives of this supreme "kingdom-come" prayer. Tertullian contrasts prayer before the coming of Christ and after His coming, highlighting what mighty things prayer can now do:

> *Of old, prayer was able to rescue from fire and beasts and hunger, even before it received its perfection from Christ. How much greater then is the power of Christian prayer. No longer does prayer bring an angel of comfort to the heart of a fiery furnace, or close up the mouths of lions, or transport to the hungry food from the fields. No longer does it remove all sense of pain by the grace it wins for others. But it gives the armor of patience to those who suffer, who feel pain, who are distressed. It strengthens the power of grace, so that faith may know what is gaining from the Lord, and understand what it is suffering for the name of God.*
>
> *In the past, prayer was able to bring down punishment, rout armies, withhold the blessing of rain. Now, however, the prayer of the just turns aside the whole anger of God, keeps vigil for its enemies, pleads for persecutors. . . . Prayer is the one thing that can conquer God. But Christ has willed that it should work no evil, and has given it all power over good.*

Its only art is to call back the souls of the dead from the very journey into death, to give strength to the weak, to heal the sick, to exorcise the possessed, to open prison cells, to free the innocent from their chains. Prayer cleanses from sin, drives away temptations, stamps out persecutions, comforts the faint-hearted, gives new strength to the courageous, brings travelers safely home, calms the waves, confounds robbers, feeds the poor, overrules the rich, lifts up the fallen, supports those who are falling, sustains those who stand firm.[2]

When prayed in the name of Christ, there is nothing that this prayer cannot accomplish. We engage with all of life. We neglect no area of the Christian world. Praying this revolutionary prayer gives us assurance that we are asking according to the revealed will of God, and therefore it fills us with boldness to ask and with confidence to believe that God will both hear and answer our pleas.

Kingdom-Come Prayer Today

1. Review the seven priorities of the Lord's Prayer. Choose one petition and compare it with your present prayer life. Do you hear the trumpets of revolution sounding?

2. Are you praying in the way Jesus taught us to pray? Don't just think it over. Pray it through with Jesus. Let Him be your prayer teacher as He was with His twelve disciples.

THE KING'S PASSION FOR A HOUSE OF PRAYER

Jesus confronts His people and draws a line in the sand

It was business as usual at the temple when Jesus arrived at the scene. Herod's magnificent temple and operations were functioning like clockwork. It was Passover and all Israel had come to Jerusalem to celebrate the mighty works of God, His rescue of Jacob's children from Egypt's Pharaoh. While most people arrived to worship and experience the communion of saints, others came to make a quick denarius exchanging currencies or selling animals for sacrifice. The religious establishment made room for both. However, something unexpected was about to happen. A disruptive presence was set to enter the temple precincts and overturn the existing order.

Consider the turmoil surrounding Jesus coming to the temple in Jerusalem. Early in the day on that first Palm Sunday, Jesus descended from the Mount of Olives, and all heaven broke loose.

Disciples and children crowded the gates and surrounded the city with loud hosannas. When commanded to stop their singing, Jesus said, "I tell you, if these were silent, the very stones would cry out" (Luke 19:40).

Then as the crowd came over the crest of the mountain, Jerusalem entered into full view, and the procession halted. Overlooking Jerusalem, Jesus wept for the city. Under the bustle of preparations for feast and festivities, there was a terrible emptiness—the rulers and people of the city failed to recognize the coming of their king. Rather than take offense, Jesus was overcome with sorrow. He wept for Jerusalem. He foresaw the consequences. With tears He prophesied, "They will not leave one stone upon another in you, because you did not know the time of your visitation" (Luke 19:44).

After this time of lament, the procession passed through the Kidron Valley and up toward the city walls. While the children continued their loud singing, Jesus entered and surveyed the temple.

Herod's glorious structure rivaled Solomon's temple, in which daily sacrifices were offered, and priests and Levites were consecrated to the liturgy and service. Yet Jesus' eye pierced through the gathering crowds and discerned a disturbing reality. While Jewish people were embraced and welcomed to pray, foreigners were consigned to a distant court and even made to pass through a commercial blockade in order to pray to God. God intended Israel to be a light for the nations and a place of prayer for all peoples. Jesus saw the exact opposite and He was deeply troubled.

As Jesus looked over Jerusalem, He recognized that this temple blockade revealed something terribly wrong in the heart of the leaders, priests, and people. In ritual and ceremony they imagined themselves to honor God. In fact, they were dishonoring God by ignoring those outside of Israel. God's honor was at stake, and

Jesus' actions reflected His passionate jealousy for His Father. This kind of jealousy is good. What child could remain unmoved if his or her father were being misrepresented or maligned? Similarly, every true believer has a burning desire to see God honored. This kind of jealousy is at the heart of what it means to love God and follow Christ. If we want to experience revolution, we will embrace His passion for making His house a house of prayer.

GOD'S PASSION FOR THE NATIONS

Almost a millennium earlier, in order that the entire world might hear of God's fame and declare His glory, God had His people build a temple to be the place of His "holy habitation." His intent was to provide a welcoming place for foreigners from every nation to stream in and offer up worship-filled prayers of thanksgiving:

> The foreigners who join themselves to the LORD,
>   to minister to him, to love the name of the LORD,
>   and to be his servants,
> everyone who keeps the Sabbath and does not profane it,
>   and holds fast my covenant—
> these I will bring to my holy mountain,
>   and make them joyful in my house of prayer . . .
> for my house shall be called a house of prayer
>   for all peoples.
>
> ISAIAH 56:6–7

God's zeal for His own glory and His plan for a worldwide church come together in this vision of a house of prayer. The temple must be a house of prayer for the nations or it will miss out on God's purpose. The temple must have gates open to the surrounding world or it will not fulfill God's vision.

God did not choose Israel to be His people to the exclusion of others; He chose Israel for the sake of the nations. As God said to Abraham, the spiritual father of Israel, "In your offspring shall all the nations of the earth be blessed" (Gen. 22:18). More than a millennium later, through the prophet Isaiah, the Lord echoed this promise, describing a day when all peoples will join in praying and worshiping God:

> I will send some of those who survive to the nations . . .
> and to the distant islands that have not heard of my fame
> or seen my glory. They will proclaim my glory among the
> nations. And they will bring all your people, from all the
> nations, to my holy mountain in Jerusalem as an offering to
> the LORD. . . .
> . . . From one New Moon to another and from one
> Sabbath to another, all mankind will come and bow
> down before me."
> **ISAIAH 66:19–20, 23 NIV**

Israel's divine calling was clear: rescued by God, they were to announce His royal splendor and gather the nations into His temple.

And so as we see Jesus enter Jerusalem, we see God's response to how Israel had defied that divine calling.

JESUS REVEALED HIS HOLY PASSION

This Palm Sunday was no ordinary day and this was no ordinary visit to the temple. This was Jesus' day of reckoning. He would measure the temple practices by the yardstick of prayer and hospitality to the outsider. Honoring God means honoring those outside the fold, and so Jesus let loose with a torrent of jealousy for God's intent to build a house of prayer.

When Jesus entered Jerusalem and surveyed the activity at the temple, He saw that fellow Jews had gathered from "every nation under heaven" (Acts 2:5) to keep the feast and remember their momentous deliverance from Egypt. If ever there was an opportunity to invite and host those who did not know about God's fame and glory, this was it. Jesus had every reason to expect to see temple doors wide open and the whole city thronging with foreigners who wanted to know more about God's fame.

He found just the opposite—a far cry from God's intended "joyful house of prayer." Instead of open doors, the temple gates were crowded with commerce. Foreigners were hindered by the chaotic, mercenary proceedings—merchants had erected kiosks at the temple entrances to offer foreign-exchange money-changing services and to sell livestock to visitors for their temple sacrifices. These seekers of God were made to feel like customers rather than guests. They were treated as commodities rather than worshipers.

If foreigners managed to navigate this temple-entry turmoil, what they found, instead of an inviting place to pray, was a designated fenced-off court far removed from the temple's worship center.[1]

Jesus was furious, literally "eaten up" with jealousy for God (see John 2:16–17), and He drew a hard line in the sand. Luke records how Jesus responded: "He entered the temple and began to drive out those who sold, saying to them, 'It is written, "My house shall be a house of prayer," but you have made it a den of robbers'" (Luke 19:45–46).

This was Jesus as we had never seen Him! This was Jesus as Judge. Righteous anger had been building in His spirit—it had to erupt. No longer weeping, Jesus came by storm—He loosed the judgment of God upon those who had corrupted the temple courts and burdened would-be worshipers. In John's account we read: "Making a whip of cords, he drove them all out of the temple, with the sheep and oxen. And he poured out the coins of the money-changers and overturned their tables" (John 2:15).

Jesus' actions fulfilled Malachi's prophesy of the ultimate visitation and purifying of the temple by the "messenger of the covenant":

> Behold, I send my messenger, and he will prepare the way before me. And the Lord whom you seek will suddenly come to his temple; and the messenger of the covenant in whom you delight, behold, he is coming, says the LORD of hosts. But who can endure the day of his coming, and who can stand when he appears? For he is like a refiner's fire and like fullers' soap.
>
> **MALACHI 3:1–2**

Jesus scattered the purveyors of greed. He was the refiner's fire, purifying His people in cleansing, white-hot anger. On this day, Jesus drew a line in the sand—from now on insiders will be left out and outsiders brought in. Unlike previous revivals, after this cleansing, there would be no return to the old ways. Christ, as Lord and Judge, gave verdict and pronounced judgment. The people of God were weighed and found wanting. Israel was supposed to share the kingdom; instead the kingdom would be taken from them and given to others, at least for a time.[2] Soon, the old temple would be reduced to ruins, and a new temple, made of living stones, would rise from the rubble.

Christ's reckoning was based on a single factor: He measured and weighed His temple by the measure of prayer. Above all and before all, God's house must be a house of prayer for all nations. And so we too must ask ourselves, "Is Jesus still drawing the same line in the sand today?"

HOW DOES THIS APPLY TO THE CHURCH TODAY?

Many times I have pondered this watershed event. One day it dawned on me to ask, "Is Jesus drawing the same line in the sand today?" Jesus' words and actions are clear. On that day, He measured the church. He said, in essence, "Build My house of prayer for all peoples. If you fail to do this, you are missing your role in the advance of the kingdom." It seems inescapable logic to consider that if it was true for the church of that day, it must be true for the church today. The line in the sand remains. Jesus is still telling His church to build a house of prayer. He is still calling, "Open your doors to the nations and build My house of prayer. As you do, you will be fulfilling your Father's purpose and promise."

This is not a theoretical issue. The urgency of Jesus' words and actions should challenge every believer. Too often, we are afflicted with the same malady Jesus encountered at the temple: a prayerless indifference to the fate of those outside. To underline the urgent importance of Jesus' words and actions, we must ask ourselves, "If Jesus were to come suddenly to our churches today, would He find that we welcome our lost neighbor to experience God in His house of prayer? Would He be pleased with our mission efforts? Or would He find us busy with meetings, attendance, cliques, and finances? Would He commend us or overturn the tables of our commerce and busyness?"

One day soon Jesus will return and visit His people, and He will divide the church based on her jealousy for God and faithfulness to His mission. Even now our risen King weighs the works of the churches. In blinding purity and righteousness, Jesus always holds court with the people of God. With piercing eyes ablaze, He searches hearts and minds to find if His people remain true to Him with all their hearts (see Rev. 2:18ff).

From the events at the temple on Palm Sunday, we learn that

the call to invite believers to get to know and love God through prayer is not just a good idea or a mere sidebar highlighting a biblical priority. Becoming a house of prayer for the nations is at the very heart of the church's kingdom mission, because it is at the very heart of our King. As leaders and people, we must pray passionately and persistently for the nations to hear of God's fame.

HOW TO START BUILDING JESUS' HOUSE OF PRAYER

To become Jesus' house of prayer, we must first examine our own hearts and practices. Are our prayers and activities too focused on just getting people to church and paying the bills? Or are we deeply engaged and passionate about God's plan to bring the nations into a saving and prayerful relationship with Him? Are we faithful in reaching the world for Christ? Are we building a house of prayer for *all* peoples?

I am not pointing fingers here. I have been a pastor for decades, and I understand that the pressures of leading a church, building its membership, and paying the bills never go away. Many times I have lost sight of God's priorities and have had to repent. God always hears my prayer and sets me back on track with His priority.

But what does it look like to build a house of prayer? From day one, when we first planted Grace Vancouver Church in 1999, we were always deep in prayer and deep in mission. Through many trials and errors, fits and starts, the Lord of the Harvest taught us several practical things about building His house of prayer.

For example, we called our midweek groups "Prayer Fellowships." We met to pray for the church, for the city, and for one another. After a relaxing time of fellowship over a meal, we shared a Bible teaching that led us to prayer. We trained our leaders to pray and to train others in prayer. Some of our groups had a number of seekers attending—including international students and new immigrants. One of these groups met in our home. One evening as we went to prayer, I looked around and noticed Japanese, Chinese, Korean, and Turkish faces. I thought it helpful and offered that each person could pray in their own language. After a few prayed in that way, Brooklyn, a Turkish woman, covered her eyes and cried profusely. Concerned, I asked, "Are you okay?"

"Yes," she said. "I am just very happy. In my country no one is allowed to pray publicly in their own language. We are told to pray memorized prayers in Arabic." Brooklyn proceeded to pray a thankful and worshipful prayer to our heavenly Father.

We also posted invitations in various language and ESL schools. Several people joined us and our church choir became a wonderful multiethnic concert of voices. Often these newcomers were just getting to know English. We had several godly worship leaders who shepherded, befriended, and prayed with and for them. As they learned the rich words of biblical choruses and hymns, their minds and hearts became enlightened. They were not only learning to sing in English, they were getting to know God.

Other prayer meetings became mini-houses of prayer for those previously outside the kingdom. For example, three young men met each week in the church office's lobby to pray together and to share what opportunities they'd had to talk with others about Christ. One day a man peered in the glass entry door and saw these three praying. He asked if he could join them. They warmly welcomed him in and the three became four. Over several months, they developed a praying friendship and watched as heart changes became a reality. At one point in their meetings, the man confessed he was getting over heroin addiction. The vulnerability with which he shared a difficult part of his past served to encouraged the others and deepen their bonds.

After a few more months, this man approached me and asked to be baptized. I was excited but wanted to make sure he understood the commitment he was making, so I asked why he wanted to be baptized. He told me, "I have been learning how to pray by meeting every week with three other men and getting to know them. I've also been reading the book they gave me—*Journey in Prayer*. I now know what it means to be a Christian, and I want to follow Christ."

There is a lesson here for all of us: not only is prayer a wonderful way to bring non-Christians before the Father, but just getting to know someone and praying with them is a wonderful way to share Jesus.

Another lesson we learned was through an elderly couple, Ed and Anne Wiens, who became full-time missionaries to the diverse international people in our community. The Wiens always had one or two students boarding with them. They invited every international and new immigrant visitor to their home for weekly meals, Bible study, and prayer. For years, until their health began to fail, they also invited the student to bring another international friend along for Thanksgiving, Christmas, and Easter dinners, as well as other celebrations. Happy guests filled the living room. Several of our younger gifted leaders joined in to help. This home became a wonderful house of prayer for all peoples, with many joyful stories of salvation.

Jesus loves His creation, but He is not a humanitarian. Jesus' actions are driven by a passion for God's glory.

We have learned that for heart transformation to occur, we need to take time to fast and pray for God to give us His heart and love for those who don't know Him. Like Jesus, we need to see that each and every unbeliever is lost and hurting at his or her core (see Matt. 9:36). If God is missing, so is lasting hope and real joy. As we pray, Jesus' zeal for God's fame becomes internalized and our affections pivot to the glory of God, a love for the nations, and a passion for prayer.

Zeal for God comes first. Jesus loves His creation, but He is not a humanitarian. Jesus' actions are driven by a passion for God's glory (see Matt. 16:23). Likewise, the more we are jealous for God, the more we will be moved with a passion for God's glory, to reach and serve a lost world. Zeal for God's name is the wellspring of that passion.

PRAY ABOUT PRAYER

We need to weigh our individual and corporate practices by Christ's standard. It will do immeasurable good to ask some important questions:

- How can we provide multiple gatherings of all kinds, from small to congregation-wide, in order to build a house of prayer for the nations?
- If deep prayer is missing from our churches and our lives, we must ask what has replaced prayer. This means examining our motives as well as our actions.
- In what specific ways have we made attendance data and financial metrics higher priorities than prayer and hospitality?

As a recovering felon in these matters, I know the pressures are great, and we need united prayer to turn our hearts outward. Rather than excusing us, sin in this area is a call to repentance.

For prayer to permeate all we do, we first need to examine

our meetings. If honest searching reveals that we have become "business-like" and self-directed in our planning sessions, we need to start over—begin a meeting with prayer and insert prayer throughout. We often practice a fifty-fifty principle: first we begin with prayer, then we move to an item of business or discussion, then we pray about this item before going on to the next matter on the agenda. When we repent and replace, God forgives us, He renews our spirits, and prayer becomes central to all of ministry, mission, and life.

Becoming a praying church or praying mission is not something that happens automatically. Just as we need training and discipleship in studying the Word, we equally need to be trained in prayer. We need to make disciples through prayer.

Perhaps the greatest progress is made when parents return to the "family altar," and teach their children the Word and prayer. Children learn to pray by praying. In this way, mothers and fathers raise up a new generation of prayer leaders.

Prayer groups for missions here and abroad also go a long way to building a house of prayer for the nations. We can be part of prayer revolution by praying intentionally for international students who are so often receptive to the gospel. We must also pray for the persecuted church. As we do, we will be praying for a mighty advance of the kingdom.[3] And we can pray for the Muslim world, where God is doing a great work of salvation.[4]

Again and again, we must ask if we have opened our doors to would-be God-worshipers or let our churches become ingrown and insular. Vast opportunities lie before us. Thousands of people from hundreds of nations, including new immigrants, refugees, and international students, are streaming into our cities, often open and willing for us to introduce them to Christ. In our two church-planting experiences, we have found that when people host newcomers in homes, invite them to fellowship activities, take them on outings, take them to church, and introduce them to Christian music, they experience long-lasting joy and deep friendships. Without any pressure, these newcomers are glad to accept an invitation to go to church. In fact, they often do not need to be asked at all. They just want to go and explore the story of Jesus.

Becoming a house of prayer is not an onerous obligation. It is the key to a joyous Christian life and thriving church fellowship. The greatest joy in heaven is when a single sinner repents and is found by the Savior (see Luke 15:7). Jesus came to save a world and He sends each of us to take His message to every nation. As we obey, Jesus will bless our every word and deed, and promises to be with us in presence, authority, and power (see Matt. 28:16–20).

Get to know your neighbors, hit the streets, and invite outsiders in. Build Jesus' house of prayer and you will further the prayer revolution and will experience His fullness of joy within you (John 15:11).

Kingdom-Come Prayer Today

1. As a believer, you are considered to be God's temple or dwelling (see Eph. 2:19–22). Are you busy building your personal life (house, income, security), or are you opening doors of hospitality and kindness? In light of that, mark where you would place yourself on the following spectrum:

Building my own house <-----------------------------> Building a house of prayer for the nations

If you are a church leader, evaluate your church or mission in the same way.

Building a house
  for attendance   <----------------------------->   Building
    and giving   a house
of prayer

2. Take some time to fast and pray with Jesus. Ask Him to guide you in becoming "a dwelling place," a house of prayer for the nations, in which God lives by His Spirit (Eph. 2:21). Write two or three practices to move you forward.

3. Get together with others to pray and discuss: "How can we begin to become a house of prayer?"

The Moravian Awakening (1727)

One of the longest lasting prayer and mission movements began with the Moravian Awakening in 1727 and continued for one hundred years. In 1722, Count Nikolaus von Zinzendorf founded the Herrnhut settlement with diverse religious refugees from surrounding countries. The makeup included Moravian, Lutheran, Reformed, and Anabaptist believers. There was little sense of power or unity in the fellowship. Things turned sour and Zindendorf lamented that the group was splintered along denominational lines. Arguments entered around contentious topics like baptism, sanctification, and predestination.

Zindendorf sought to counter these divisions by drawing up a document focusing on the evangelical agreements between the groups. May 12, 1727, marks a historic beginning as all parties signed the document. As if to cement this agreement, on July 22, many of the community promised to join in regular prayer and worship.

A great turn around was signaled when, on August 5, Zindendorf and around a dozen others held an all-night prayer meeting filled with worship and heart-rending repentance.

God heard and on August 13 poured out abundant grace and power from the throne room. A mighty work of God had begun. "No one present could tell exactly what happened on that Wednesday morning . . . at the specially called Communion service," but "Zinzendorf described it as 'a sense of the nearness of

Christ.' . . . Many of them decided to set aside certain times for continued earnest prayer."[5]

Zinzendorf was overwhelmed with a vision of Jesus' love, and years later as he recalled their experience, he stated, "O head so full of bruises, so full of pain and scorn. In this view of the man of sorrows and acquainted with grief, their hearts told them that He would be their patron and their priest who was at once changing their tears into oil of gladness and their misery into happiness."[6]

"A spirit of prayer was immediately evident in the fellowship and continued throughout that 'golden summer of 1727,'" and "on August 27 . . . twenty-four men and twenty-four women covenanted to spend one hour each day in scheduled prayer. . . . others enlisted in 'hourly intercession.'"[7] Unbidden, even children gathered to pray.

In prayer and the Spirit, the Moravians sent out missionaries, and news of the revival spread to surrounding nations. Over the next twenty-five years, from that little village, one hundred missionaries traveled to the most difficult and destitute regions of the world to preach Christ. And for more than a hundred years, members of the Moravian Church continued in the "hourly intercession."[8]

PART 2

KINGDOM PRAYER
BREAKS OUT

HOW CHRIST'S ASCENSION BRINGS A NEW DAY FOR PRAYER

We pray in union with the exalted Christ

As Jesus ascended to heaven, He issued a call to prayer and a promise of power (see Acts 1:4, 8). As Jesus commanded them, His disciples prayed and waited for His promised Spirit. All of a sudden, gale force winds blew. Flames spread through a crowd. Earthquakes shook foundations. The power manifested at Pentecost signaled a new day for the world and a new day for prayer.

The narrative of the early church reveals overwhelming evidence that the volume of answered prayer escalated from intermittent stream to cascading waterfall. In Old Testament history, God periodically and occasionally revealed His presence in miracles. After the ascension, great works of God burst forth with expressive fullness, like flower blossoms in springtime. Winter was long gone. Timid people became courageous as lions, shouting long-kept secrets of heaven from the housetops. Believing prayer gave birth to extraordinary answers, including great numbers coming to faith.

In this new day of prayer, God encourages to ask away! "Everyone who asks receives; the one who seeks finds; and to the one who knocks, the door will be opened" (Luke 11:10 NIV). Jesus repeated the promise again and again: "If you ask me anything in my name, I will do it" (John 14:13–14; 15:7; 16:26).

God has always been a prayer-answering God. In countless promises and innumerable events, the Old Testament assures every believer that God hears the prayers of His beloved children. The psalmist celebrated, "O you who hear prayer, to you shall all flesh come" (Ps. 65:2) and, "I love the LORD, because he has heard my voice and my pleas for mercy. Because he inclined his ear to me, therefore I will call on him as long as I live" (Ps. 116:1–2).

Yet following Christ's resurrection, prayer offered in Jesus' name took asking and receiving into unlimited realms. Now that salvation had been won at the cross and Jesus is seated in royal power and glory, we could argue that the chief purpose of prayer is that God answers and gives what we ask for. For example, in the Gospel of John, Jesus foreshadowed the coming day of answered prayer; no less than six times He proclaimed unbounded promises for those who pray:

- "Whoever believes in me will also do the works that I do; and greater works than these will he do, because I am going to the Father. Whatever you ask in my name, this I will do, that the Father may be glorified in the Son" (John 14:12–13).
- "If you ask me anything in my name, I will do it" (John 14:14).
- "If you abide in me, and my words abide in you, ask whatever you wish, and it will be done for you. By this my Father is

glorified, that you bear much fruit and so prove to be my disciples" (John 15:7–8).

- "You did not choose me, but I chose you and appointed you that you should go and bear fruit and that your fruit should abide, so that whatever you ask the Father in my name, he may give it to you" (John 15:16).

- "In that day you will ask nothing of me. Truly, truly, I say to you, whatever you ask of the Father in my name, he will give it to you. Until now you have asked nothing in my name. Ask, and you will receive, that your joy may be full" (John 16:23–24).

- "In that day you will ask in my name, and I do not say to you that I will ask the Father on your behalf; for the Father himself loves you, because you have loved me and have believed that I came from God" (John 16:26–27).

Jesus assigned no limits to prayer being answered, only guidelines. For example, He promised answers to our prayers as we ask in Jesus' name, as we ask for the Father to be glorified, as we abide in Jesus, and as we keep His commandments. The environment of answered prayer is redemptive, not transactional.

Our prayers will be answered because Jesus is both Redeemer and King. His priesthood is a royal priesthood. His rule is a redemptive rule (see Ps. 110:4, Heb. 5:9). In days of weakness and affliction, every believer cries out for mercy and for power. Jesus is abundantly able to answer. As our eternal Redeemer, Jesus willingly grants complete pardon and new righteousness. As our forever King, Jesus gladly pours out a torrent of ascension power.

As we align with our Redeemer-King and enter a new day of prayer revolution, we keep our eyes focused on four key elements that characterize ascension prayer.

KEY #1: OUR PRAYERS OF FAITH FOCUS
ON AN ENTHRONED KING

Christian prayer is radically distinct from all other prayer. When a Christian prays, he has an exalted King ever in mind. Christian prayer rejoices in Christ's ascension and participates in Christ's authority over heaven and earth.

Sometimes we forget to whom we pray. Attend prayer meetings or listen to Sunday morning prayers, and we might imagine Jesus as a heavenly housekeeper cleaning up humankind's problems, whose job it is to keep the world tidy and running smoothly. This kind of prayer flows from the mind of humans and not from the throne of Christ.

> **Men and women of prayer do not derive their prayer requests from watching the news. Rather, believers get their prayer agenda from studying Scripture and gazing at a risen Savior.**

Men and women of prayer do not derive their prayer requests from watching the news—the world cares little for the purposes of God. Kingdom advance, the essence of history, is edited out. Rather, believers get their prayer agenda from studying Scripture and gazing at a risen Savior.

I find when I immerse myself in the teaching of Christ's ascension, I experience wonderful consequences. The more time I spend studying the ascension and its relation to prayer, the more I realize how pervasive and powerful this teaching is. The New Testament is incandescent with this reality.

Previously, I had been selling my heart short and missing out on what is perhaps the chief joy and power of prayer. Blinkered, I was unable to fully grasp the magnificent promises flowing from the throne of our exalted Lord. My prayers were constricted to the here and now—preoccupied with my little world and those around me. Feeding on the reality of Christ's present rule and reign, my world of prayer grew larger. With new confidence, my asking turned to interceding, my requests reaching far beyond narrow boundaries of self. For example, I now love to pray for the persecuted church. When we pray, we do something meaningful and effective about the imprisonment, exile, and shame that our brothers and sisters bear for Christ. I can't help but bring this emphasis into various prayer meetings.

I now eagerly search and study the many passages relating to Christ's ascension. Waking to this reality fills my morning devotions with new light and joyful songs that celebrate the ascension. I rejoice over singing mighty hymns like "Rejoice the Lord Is King," "All Hail the Power of Jesus' Name," and "Crown Him with Many Crowns."

On the other hand, when I lose sight of Christ, forgetting He has already defeated every enemy on the cross, I become anxious and timid in prayer. I imagine a contest between good and evil, a kind of spiritual tug of war, and ask God to do His best to give me victory over sin, death, and the devil in my life and world. I walk away unchanged and unanswered. If you think about it, this is the way prayer works for any Christian: focus on a problem, or the present darkness, or on self, and your power and confidence in prayer deflates like air pressure from a badly leaking tire.

KEY #2: OUR PRAYERS SHARE IN THE PRESENT RULE AND REIGN OF JESUS

Now and forevermore, Jesus sits in triumph on heaven's throne. He is the sole and absolute ruler of heaven and earth. While we can remember Jesus on the cross, it is wrong to imagine Him still hanging there. At His resurrection, Jesus told Mary not to linger at the tomb but to go and tell the others He had risen and was soon ascending to the Father (see John 20:17). To picture Jesus as He is today, envision Him as the risen Ruler, seated on a glorious throne with all heaven and earth at His feet, "far above all rule and authority and power and dominion, and above every name that is named, not only in this age but also in the one to come" (Eph. 1:21).

As we pray, our eyes of faith are fixed on Christ as He exists *now*, in unimaginable splendor and blinding glory: "His eyes were like a flame of fire, his feet were like burnished bronze, refined in a furnace, and his voice was like the roar of many waters. . . . From his mouth came a sharp two-edged sword, and his face was like the sun shining in full strength" (Rev. 1:14–16).

We have even more good news. Jesus does not keep His conquering power and authority to Himself. In answer to our prayers, He pours out the Holy Spirit from on high into our hearts, so we might experience "what is the immeasurable greatness of his power toward us who believe, according to the working of his great might that he worked in Christ when he . . . seated him at his right hand in the heavenly places" (Eph. 1:19–20).

Problems that seemed so daunting diminish in proportion to our experience of His indwelling power. For example, when you are suffering under a strained relationship and it seems impossible to mend, do not lose hope. Humbly ask Christ to fill you within. The very power and hope of heaven will fill your heart and you will begin to experience hope within and patience for the other. The healing between the two of you has already begun.

KEY #3: OUR PRAYERS BRING ASCENSION REALITIES INTO THE WORLD

The Scriptures are shameless in references to the present power of Christ in the life and prayers of a believer. The apostle Paul prayed that God would fill His people with a consciousness of His resurrection power and Christ's ascension authority:

> that the God of our Lord Jesus Christ, the Father of glory, may give you the Spirit of wisdom and of revelation . . . that you may know . . . what is the immeasurable greatness of his power toward us who believe, according to the working of his great might that he worked in Christ when he raised him from the dead and seated him at his right hand in the heavenly places, far above all rule and authority and power and dominion.
>
> EPHESIANS 1:17–21

Ascension prayer is a matter of experiencing Christ's power. Domestic prayers for the status quo betray an emaciated view of Jesus and His coming kingdom. When we "under-conceive" Jesus, we miss out on the power of His triumphant ascension.

Praying into Jesus' power and authority is more than an exercise of our imagination. As we pray, we are supernaturally united with Him, and seated with Him in heavenly places (see Eph. 2:6). His power is "toward us" and "within us" (Eph. 1:19, 3:20). What fuels our every prayer is our supernatural union with Him: "You have been filled in him, who is the head of all rule and authority" (Col. 2:10).

I have found that when I abide in the present reality of Christ's rule and reign, the entire temperament of my prayer changes. I come to the Father burdened with care and weak with worry. However, when the Savior of the world inhabits my prayers, I immediately feel a sense of boundless hope. I tire of self and move to boldly interceding for others. Jesus did not change; I did.

If prayer becomes boring and self-centered, it is because we have forgotten to fix our eyes on Jesus. Once we recall that we are united to Him in His present power and glory, we become what we pray. Pray about our worries and we become worriers. Pray to the King, and we become like the King.

This is not just talking yourself into something. You can tell when you are praying in the presence and power of the living Christ. As you contemplate the many facets of Christ's present majesty, your prayers will spontaneously burst into praise: "Worthy is the Lamb who was slain, to receive power and wealth and wisdom and might and honor and glory and blessing!" (Rev. 5:12). Joyous days of effective ministry begin with full-throated, unrestrained praise of our Redeemer-King.

At times as we gather to pray for extended hours, we become deeply aware that the King is in our midst. A hush falls over all present, so words are not needed. Abiding in the presence of Christ is perhaps the greatest joy of prayer. At the best times, in the midst of quiet waiting, a kind of Pentecost breaks out; effortlessly our voices unite to give thanks and praise to Christ. I have experienced prayer gatherings when it seemed those gathered could not stop praying if they wanted to. The Spirit takes over and orchestrates a timeless concert of intercession and supplication.

KEY #4: OUR PRAYERS EXPRESS THE RULE AND REIGN OF CHRIST OVER THE NATIONS

In the previous chapter, we watched Jesus cleanse the temple. His entire life purpose, and reason for dying, is for all the nations to be blessed through Him. When Christ declared, "All authority in heaven and on earth has been given to me" (Matt. 28:18), He announced the crowning accomplishment of His finished work on the cross. From the day of His ascension, Christ rules over the rulers of the earth. As Psalm 2:9 and Revelation 2:27 and 19:15 tell us, at this very moment, Jesus governs the nations with a rod of iron. Like a mighty charioteer who restrains and guides his battle horses with bit and bridle, Christ steers the nations to His desired destiny. The outcome is fixed and certain: the day is quickly coming when every knee will bow in worship to the true, ascended King.

In bold awareness of Christ's present rule, we do not pray merely for an end to war, trouble, and for world peace, for Jesus said, "I have not come to bring peace" (Matt. 10:34). We pray for kings and rulers, that they might submit to His rule and carry out His saving purposes. We do not pray for order in the world—we pray for a new world order.

As Paul wrote,

> First of all, then, I urge that supplications, prayers, intercessions, and thanksgivings be made for all people, for kings and all who are in high positions, that we may lead a peaceful and quiet life, godly and dignified in every way. This is good, and it is pleasing in the sight of God our Savior, who desires all people to be saved and to come to the knowledge of the truth.
>
> 1 TIMOTHY 2:1–4

In these comprehensive words, Paul redefined congregational prayer—rejecting prayers for domestic complacency and replacing them with intercession for national renewal. Consider a few key phrases:

First of all we must pray for our land. Intercessory prayer is the first priority for the gathered church, and a great sin to neglect.

For all people, for kings and all who are in high positions—those in authority. Our prayers should include all those who rule, including politicians, judges and courts, media leaders, teachers, and policy makers.

That we may lead a peaceful and quiet life, godly and dignified in every way. Politicians, educators, the judiciary, and media leaders have a greater obligation than keeping civic peace and order. Promoting reverence for God, and encouraging virtuous and devout lives by enacting laws that are filled with truth and justice is the assigned task of every leader.

This is good, and it is pleasing in the sight of God our Savior, who desires all people to be saved. Our leaders and rulers are appointed the work of keeping doors open for the church of Jesus Christ to freely and without hindrance proclaim the Good News in public and in private. Needless to say, this is a stunning rebuke of the secular state, which forbids any form of witnessing to Christ in public service, including courts, schools, and hospitals—places where the message of Christ is most needed.

Real democracy places God at the center. Though we may vote or hire someone to lead, they will ultimately render account to God. As Paul said, "There is no authority except from God, and those that exist have been instituted by God" (Rom. 13:1; 14:10). We must hold our leaders accountable to the people who elect them, but even more importantly, we must pray they will reverence the One who ultimately appoints them to their office.

There are other ways our prayers express the rule and reign of our ascended Christ:

Our Prayers Partner with Jesus When We Pray for Justice

We also pray into the present reign of Christ when we intercede and work for justice and righteousness in our land. At present and until the day He returns, Jesus is executing justice and bringing liberty throughout the world. As the prophet Isaiah wrote:

> I have put my Spirit upon him;
>> he will bring forth justice to the nations.
> He will not cry aloud or lift up his voice,
>> or make it heard in the street;
> a bruised reed he will not break,
>> and a faintly burning wick he will not quench;
>> he will faithfully bring forth justice.
> He will not grow faint or be discouraged
>> till he has established justice in the earth;
>> and the coastlands wait for his law.
>
> ISAIAH 42:1–4

When they pray and work for justice, Christians align themselves with the present rule and reign of Jesus. God hears our prayers for the oppressed and authorizes us to carry out the rebuilding of the city from the ground up:

> Then you shall call, and the LORD will answer;
>> you shall cry, and he will say, "Here I am." . . .
> If you pour yourself out for the hungry
>> and satisfy the desire of the afflicted . . .
> And the LORD will guide you continually . . .
> And your ancient ruins shall be rebuilt;
>> you shall raise up the foundations of many generations;
> you shall be called the repairer of the breach,
>> the restorer of streets to dwell in.
>
> ISAIAH 58:9–12

Jesus does not cry out or lift His voice, but His people do—in prayer! We raise a cry to God to defend the captive, enslaved, trafficked, and oppressed of the world. We do not have to avoid the bad news because we can't do anything about it. Every time we get on our knees to pray for the oppressed—for refugees, for the poor and destitute, for trafficked women and children, for the persecuted church—we partner with Jesus. Though we may not always be able to assist in other ways, when we pray for justice, we help in the most important way! Our heartfelt cries for justice please the King and we are participating in His grand and certain plan to set free every captive of sin and injustice.

Our Prayers Are Alive with Anticipation of the Return of the King

In the present day things seem bleak in the world and hope is in short supply. Not only fiery street evangelists see the coming of the end; apocalyptic images fill our collective vision of the future. Movies and television shows forebode a catastrophic and cannibalistic world. Consider *Hunger Games, Night of the Living Dead, Planet Z, Legion, Twilight, Mad Max,* and *The Book of Eli,* among countless more examples. Purveyors of entertainment feed the coming generations a vision of death and despair.

For the worldly today, a fight for survival supplants joy in creation. Glued to news headlines, people hear loud alarms about the environment, recoil at disasters and tragedies, and are gripped by fear and distress. "Stop global warming!" "Win the war against terrorism!" "Close the borders before the world gets in!" Men, women, and children are bludgeoned with fear and left without hope and without God in the world (see Eph. 2:12). This fills every caring Christian with sorrow and moves them to passionate prayer for those who don't know the hope of Christ.

Compare this sad reality with the grand expectation of Christ's coming kingdom. What a contrast between the world's vision of the future and a believer's confident expectation! The long-awaited King is coming soon, and what a coming it will be!

> For as the lightning comes from the east and shines as far as the west, so will be the coming of the Son of Man. . . . Then all the tribes of the earth will mourn, and they will see the Son of Man coming on the clouds of heaven with power and great glory.
>
> MATTHEW 24:27, 30

As we pray, God opens the eyes of our faith, and we feel the gathering momentum. Soon, even now, clouds pregnant with justice burst open and cleanse the land. The rains of grace refresh the earth with new life. The storm passes, and a joyous new day dawns as the sun rises to an everlasting day.

Our prayer, indeed the whole Christian life, is filled with this happy expectation. Heartbreaking sorrows, trials, failures, and even sin cannot quench it. The indwelling Spirit of Christ has fixed this hope in the deepest, innermost part of our being.

A DAY OF RECKONING PRECEDES THE DAY OF RENEWAL

Jesus' first coming was in weakness and sacrifice; His second coming will be in power and judgment. He came as a lamb to die; He returns as a lion to conquer. In the closing scene of human history, Jesus dominates the horizons of heaven and earth. In hidden ways He now rules and reigns over all the world. One day soon, in blinding glory and full revelation, every eye will see Him, and everyone, even wicked men and spirits, will bow acknowledging Jesus as the everlasting King of kings and Lord of lords (see Rom.

14:11). Reckoning precedes renewal. The judgment of all who oppress and enslave the earth must happen for the earth to be set free. The glorious liberty of the sons and daughters of God requires deliverance from their captors. If the slave is to be set free, then the slave owner must first be defeated. These prayers capture God as our liberator:

> May [God] defend the cause of the poor of the people,
>> give deliverance to the children of the needy,
>> and crush the oppressor!
>
> PSALM 72:4

> From the heavens you uttered judgment;
>> the earth feared and was still,
> when God arose to establish judgment,
>> to save all the humble of the earth.
>
> PSALM 76:8–9

Yet rising out of dreadful warnings arises a beautiful invitation. The warning of judgment is simultaneously a call to repentance and faith. God takes no pleasure in the death of the wicked (Ezek. 33:11). Jesus did not come to judge the world, but to save the world (John 12:47). He desires for everyone to be saved (1 Tim. 2:4). God offers a full and free pardon to all who bow the knee to the coming King: "The Spirit and the Bride say, 'Come.' And let the one who hears say, 'Come.' And let the one who is thirsty come; let the one who desires take the water of life without price" (Rev. 22:17).

Our task is simple—we get to hand out the wedding invitations! We pray daily to be prepared for His coming. We pray daily for our neighbors—and the whole world—to come to Jesus in repentance and worship.

SIGNS THAT HIS COMING IS NEAR

How soon will the second coming be? What signs do we look for?

One sign that heralds the return of Christ is that the world starts to come apart at the seams. Our global awareness has revealed that the fabric of civilization is strained, often to the breaking point. As Isaiah wrote: "The earth is utterly broken, the earth is split apart, the earth is violently shaken. The earth staggers like a drunken man; it sways like a hut; its transgression lies heavy upon it, and it falls, and will not rise again" (24:19–20).

Another sign of Jesus' imminent return will be a growing coldness and hatefulness of the world's inhabitants toward one another, and especially toward Christians. A concerted antipathy will be poured out on God's people:

> They will deliver you up to tribulation and put you to death, and you will be hated by all nations for my name's sake. And then many will fall away and betray one another and hate one another. And many false prophets will arise and lead many astray. And because lawlessness will be increased, the love of many will grow cold.
> MATTHEW 24:9–12

Today, the persecution of believers is a worldwide reality, and the intensity is increasing. Much of the world is arrayed against Christ and His people. There is widespread persecution of Christians in the Islamic world, as well as in China, Cuba, and North Korea. Radical Hindus in India have recently banded against the cause of Christ, exiling foreign missionaries. Moreover, in the atheistic West, leaders, rulers, and policymakers in the state, judiciary, and public service institute more and more laws that ignore God's law, forbid the use of His name in public institutions, and otherwise hinder the advance of the gospel.

Psalm 2 is prophetic of our day: "Why do the nations conspire and the peoples plot in vain? The kings of the earth rise up and the rulers band together against the LORD and against his anointed" (vv. 1–2 NIV). When the nations gather together against Jesus and His people, He tells us to watch, pray, and prepare for His coming.

On the other hand a glorious sign that Jesus is near is that the world will experience a massive turning to Christ. As Jesus foretold: "This gospel of the kingdom will be proclaimed throughout the whole world as a testimony to all nations, and then the end will come" (Matt. 24:14).

This rapid expansion of the kingdom is happening now! Between 1990 and 2010 the number of Chinese Christians surged from ten million to as many as seventy million,[1] and the numbers continue to rise.[2] Doors to evangelize the Muslim world, previously closed for 1,400 years, are suddenly open. From a mere handful of believers at the turn of the century, there are now many more than two million followers of Christ in the Muslim world.[3] It is no coincidence that the International Concerts of Prayer, using tools like the *Thirty Days of Prayer for the Muslim World* guide, began in 1995. This movement has now swollen to many thousands of intercessors who pray during Ramadan for the world of Islam.[4] Similar stories of great numbers of conversions to Christ are coming out of India, Southeast Asia, Cuba, South America, and Africa.[5]

These signs lead us to greater opportunities for prayer. The world counts on us to take up the prayer revolution and boldly move forward. As we lift up our hearts and hands to God in prayer for many to be saved and to follow the King, we render the world the greatest service we can offer.

"COME, LORD JESUS!"

The excitement of Jesus coming back fills our prayers with anticipation. But also rising from this certain hope is a loud cry from our hearts. We not only anticipate the coming of Christ, we cry out for the King to come soon.

In our world today we clearly see storm clouds gathering on the horizon. Yet at the same time we see more—we lift our eyes expectantly to a brighter light. A new day is dawning. This awareness fills our prayers with an ever increasing and expectant joy.

Kingdom-Come Prayer Today

1. What do your current prayers reveal about your perspective of Jesus? Are they self-involved or God-exalting? How might you "fix your eyes" or alter your vision of Jesus so that your prayers reflect His glorified position as resurrected and exalted King?

2. Jesus told us to be filled with the Spirit. How often do you ask God to immerse you in the reality of Jesus' personal presence and power? How much of your prayers and daily life reflect this reality?

3. What difference would it make to your prayers if you fed your imagination and heart with the grand hope of Christ's imminent coming?

The Fulton Street Revival (1857)

Often revival happens in times of great spiritual and social darkness. This was the case with the New York City revival of 1857–1859. In late 1857, the stock market began to tumble. Banks failed, factories closed, and unemployment increased.

During that time, Jeremiah Lanphier, a lay leader in the Dutch Reformed church, rented a hall on Fulton Street and opened the doors for noon-hour prayer meetings.

The first day, September 23, 1857, Jeremiah prayed alone for the first half hour. By the end of the hour, six other men joined him. Two days later, when a major bank failed, nearly forty attended. On October 10, the stock market crashed, and one week later more than one hundred came to pray. Within six months, some ten thousand people gathered for daily prayer in various churches and venues throughout the city. When these places became overcrowded, churches opened their doors for morning prayer meetings.

Within three months of the start of what became known as the Fulton Street Revival, similar noon-day prayer meetings sprang up all across America: in Boston; Baltimore; Washington, D.C.; Richmond; Charleston; Savannah; Mobile; New Orleans; Vicksburg; Memphis; St. Louis; Pittsburgh; Cincinnati; Chicago; and a multitude of other cities, towns, and rural communities.

This unique awakening was all about prayer. There were no sermons or teaching. Everyday people attended and anyone was allowed to pray aloud for up to five minutes. Time was set aside to share testimonies of answered prayers—especially of friends and loved ones coming to faith in Christ. *The Presbyterian* magazine reported that, as of May 1858, nearly fifty thousand people converted to Christianity as a result of the revival.

The list of those profoundly affected by the revival include D. L. Moody, evangelist and founder of Moody Bible Institute; William Booth, the founder of the Salvation Army; the great preacher Charles H. Spurgeon; and the father of the Christian Missionary Alliance, A. B. Simpson.

5

HOW HOLY SPIRIT ADVANCES IGNITE IN PRAYER

The New Testament sets a sequence of mission

When it comes to mission strategy, we all easily agree that prayer is important. But when it comes to putting our plans into practice, few are willing to make prayer first in priority and first in sequence. A study of the powerful expansion of the early church, however, confirms the primacy of prayer. In fact, prayer initiates every advance of the kingdom.

Prayer is at the deepest core of kingdom advance. When we lose sight of this unalterable truth, we must go back and get in step with the Holy Spirit. For our strategies to be in line with God's Word, we must begin on our knees and immerse everything we do in prayer. Visions that once pulsed with life grow old and wooden unless they are forged, shaped, and reshaped in prayer.

As we pray and plan in prayer, we will be caught in the Spirit's forward momentum and carried into the mission of Christ. When we become tethered to outdated and ineffective mission strategies, only the Holy Spirit can unshackle us.

Some years ago, while working for Mission to North America, I had a defining moment—a lesson I learned in a powerful way. Driving to work in Atlanta on the I-85 South, the main north-south corridor, I was heavy with discouragement. I came to Spaghetti Junction, a complex triple-tier intersection, passing underneath several highways overhead. This junction felt like a metaphor for the many challenges hitting me from all sides over the previous months.

One of my children was going through some serious growing-up problems, and my heart was wounded for her. Intersecting with this, I was assaulted by doubts regarding the home-mission strategy I had been leading for our denomination. We were starting a lot of churches, but some of our finest pastors were failing. Colliding with this was a realization that few of our church starts were effective at reaching and serving those outside the church. We were working hard and praying some, but I couldn't shake the firm conviction that something important was missing. In the center of these troubles, I seriously considered resigning.

Somewhere between entering the junction and coming out the other side, my conflicting thoughts began to untangle. God was pointing me in a new direction. Over the next weeks it became clear. I knew I needed to change course—I needed to get back to the biblical and Holy Spirit strategy for mission. Above all else, I needed to lead in prayer. Though I was still sad, my heavy spirit began to lift.

I had been studying the book of Acts in my personal reading. I stayed there and began an intensive and in-depth study of it. I discovered that every advance of the early church—each endowment of courage for evangelism and all the fillings of power to withstand and conquer the enemy—was ignited by earnest and united prayer. In that day and ours, when it comes to the mission and call of the church, the first sign that the Holy Spirit is at work is the earnest united prayer of His people.

THE HOLY SPIRIT GIVES US A STRATEGY TO REACH THE WORLD

A survey of the Acts of the Apostles, which is first and foremost the acts of the Holy Spirit, reveals the central role of prayer in the advance and expansion of the church. When it comes to Christ's mission, prayer is a first priority and comes first in sequence. In the early church, believers met every challenge with earnest and united prayer; every advance began with a praying people. Leaders and members launched the mission in steadfast prayer (Acts 1:14; 2:1). From united prayer flowed bold and sacrificial evangelism (Acts 2:41; 4:3–4). As thousands of people were saved, new believers were enfolded into a praying community (Acts 2:42–47). When the Spirit was in charge, leaders devoted themselves to prayer and the Word (Acts 6:4). From prayer-formed fellowship flowed everything the believers needed to advance the gospel: leaders exercised church discipline (Acts 5:13–14), deployed other leaders (Acts 6:1–7), nurtured lay evangelism (Acts 8:4), and championed church planting (Acts 9:31). As believers united in prayer, the early church enjoyed explosive, joyous expansion.

The order of events in this historical record is no accident; it is how the Holy Spirit works at all times and places. If we hope to experience the powerful leading of the Holy Spirit today, we too will need to enter the flow and sequence recorded in the early church.

A SEQUENCE OF MISSION IS EMBEDDED
IN THE NEW TESTAMENT

As we study the New Testament, we see a pattern and sequence to the history of kingdom advance. The text reveals an order that is as significant as the events themselves. Luke, the author of Acts, provided the church with a pattern for future mission activity by presenting an intentional chronology. This sequence was not accidental, but normative and it consisted of five stages in chronological sequence:

1. The outpouring of Christ's power in the context of waiting prayer (Acts 1:8, 14; 2:1–4)
2. Conversion growth through bold evangelism and the preaching of Christ's resurrection (Acts 2:36–41)
3. Community formation from a harvest of new converts (Acts 2:41–47; 8:4)
4. Mobilization through leadership selection and lay development (Acts 6:1–8)
5. Multiplication through extensive church planting (Acts 9:31)

Acts Sequence of Church Multiplication

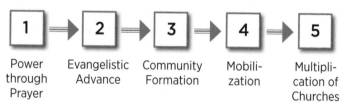

1	2	3	4	5
Power through Prayer	Evangelistic Advance	Community Formation	Mobilization	Multiplication of Churches

This order is not only normative for new missions; every church and mission that hopes for renewal and revival needs to return to this sequence. To progress in kingdom advance, we have to start over.

Let's unpack each of these stages one at a time in order to reveal the flow and symmetry of the whole.

Stage 1: Mission Progress Begins by Waiting

The first in both priority and sequence is empowerment through concerted and united prayer. The emphasis was on the disciples waiting. Jesus told them to "wait for the promise of the Father, which... 'you heard from me; for John baptized with water, but you will be baptized with the Holy Spirit not many days from now'" (Acts 1:4–5). Waiting is obedience translated into prayer.

The disciples had just seen the risen Christ. They were eager to head out, yet they must wait in prayer before proceeding. The coming battle would be hard-pitched and to-the-death, every advance met by counterattack. Jesus commanded the disciples to wait, and so they waited in earnest and united prayer: "All these with one accord were devoting themselves to prayer, together with the women and Mary the mother of Jesus, and his brothers" (Acts 1:14).

What happened next is proof of the almightiness of the ascended Christ as He answered their prayers with supernatural manifestations:

> When the day of Pentecost arrived, they were all together in one place. And suddenly there came from heaven a sound like a mighty rushing wind, and it filled the entire house where they were sitting. And divided tongues as of fire appeared to them and rested on each one of them. And they were all filled with the Holy Spirit and began to speak in other tongues as the Spirit gave them utterance.
>
> ACTS 2:1–4

When Jesus tells His followers to wait, it is no less than a cease-and-desist order. It is as though He is telling us: "Whatever you are doing . . . STOP!"

The practice of waiting on God is of utmost importance for the Christian. *Wait* is a profound and pregnant word in Scripture and in a Christian's life.

Isaiah reminds us of that importance: "The LORD waits to be gracious to you, and therefore he exalts himself to show mercy to you. . . . Blessed are all those who wait for him" (30:18) and "Since ancient times no one has heard, no ear has perceived, no eye has seen any God besides you, who acts on behalf of those who wait for him" (64:4 NIV).

When Jesus tells His followers to wait, it is no less than a cease-and-desist order. It is as though He is telling us: "Whatever you are doing . . . STOP!" Jesus issued a warning that we dare not move ahead without calibrating our plans with His: "Apart from me you can do nothing" (John 15:5). If you go ahead without waiting, you go ahead alone.

Waiting, however, is not a cessation of activity! Waiting is filled with prayer. To wait on God is to pray; to pray is to wait on God. The disciples clearly understood this, as "all these with one accord were devoting themselves to prayer" (Acts 1:14).

Waiting is both emptying and filling. To wait, we must first empty ourselves of striving ambition and self-reliance. God rebukes planning that excludes His sovereign leadership: "Ah, stubborn children . . . who carry out a plan, but not mine, and who make an alliance, but not of my Spirit" (Isa. 30:1).

Emptying makes way for filling. We not only wait for Christ's Word and power, we wait on Christ in joyous worship. Seeing Jesus ascend, the disciples worshiped Him in great joy and were continually in the temple praising God.

If there is a warning in Jesus' word to wait, it is overwhelmed by the greatness of His promise. Waiting is pregnant with expectation. As He said, "Wait . . . [and] you will receive power when the Holy Spirit has come upon you, and you will be my witnesses . . . to the end of the earth" (Acts 1:4, 8). Waiting on God is an expectant anticipation of the supernatural presence and power of Christ.

Waiting produces the greatest joys of the Christian's life and service. Those who learn to wait are continually surprised by the mighty acts of God. Overwhelmed with seeing God at work, they will never turn back to fending for themselves to make things happen. For "no ear has perceived, no eye has seen any God besides you, who acts on behalf of those who wait for him" (Isa. 64:4 NIV).

Since becoming a Christian fifty years ago, I have found it to be an invariable principle that waiting on God reverses the ratio of joy in relation to expectation. The numbers are guesswork, but I call it the 80/20 principle. Go ahead in our own plans and 80 percent of our lives will be predictable and 20 percent unexpected. Wait on Jesus in prayer and 20 percent of our lives will be predictable and 80 percent will be infused with the surprising work of the Holy Spirit.

For example, when my family and I arrived in Vancouver, British Columbia, in 1999, to plant a congregation, my wife, Caron, was praying for sexually exploited women and children. At first our prayers focused attention on the notorious "Kiddie Stroll" section of town, between Commercial and Clarke Drives, where boys and girls as young as twelve were being trafficked for early-morning Johns on their way downtown to work.

What happened soon after confirms the 80/20 principle. Within a year, leaders from a nonprofit ministry to trafficked women and their children moved into our area and started coming to the church. Eager for assistance, they quickly put us to work, helping them find and renovate a safe place for women victims in the sex industry to be protected, receive job training, and provide child care. When we pray, "coincidences" happen!

Stage 2: Prayer Empowers Bold and Effective Evangelism

Flowing from the headwaters of prayer, the second stage of the Acts model is courageous evangelism that results in a river of conversions. Peter's bold sermon provides an example of the kind of uncompromising preaching that saves souls:

> "Let all the house of Israel therefore know for certain that God has made him both Lord and Christ, this Jesus whom you crucified."
>
> Now when they heard this they were cut to the heart, and said to Peter and the rest of the apostles, "Brothers, what shall we do?" And Peter said to them, "Repent and be baptized every one of you in the name of Jesus Christ for the forgiveness of your sins, and you will receive the gift of the Holy Spirit." . . . So those who received his word were baptized, and there were added that day about three thousand souls.
>
> ACTS 2:36–38, 41

Obeying Christ, they waited. As they waited, they received power. Having received power, they witnessed—with tremendous results.

Far from being shy about numbers, the early church measured the Spirit's advance in the language of arithmetic: "There were added that day about three thousand souls" (Acts 2:41); "the number of the men came to about five thousand" (4:4); "the number of the disciples multiplied . . . and a great many of the priests became obedient to the faith" (6:7); more and more the church multiplied (9:31); "and a great many people were added to the Lord" (11:24).

In parallel language, Luke narrated how the gospel message spread with increasing momentum: "The word of God continued to increase" (6:7); "the word of God increased and multiplied" (12:24); "the word of the Lord was spreading throughout the whole region" (13:49); "the word of the Lord continued to increase and prevail mightily" (19:20).

When leaders evangelize, it is contagious. Leaders and people "were all filled with the Holy Spirit and continued to speak the word of God with boldness" (4:31). After Stephen was martyred, "those who were scattered went about preaching the word" (8:4) . . . "and the hand of the Lord was with them, and a great number who believed turned to the Lord" (11:21). Like the apostles, God's people became evangelists!

Many Christians today have the will and desire to share their faith. They know the need but are held back by fear. Prayer will bring courage. False prophets counsel Christians to stay put and stay safe: "You might offend someone." A timid flock waits for a few bold leaders to plunge into evangelism; once they dive in, members follow. Yes, some are persecuted for the cause, but this only serves to drive everyone to their knees, pleading for more power. Only the false prophets end up disappointed.

I asked a friend working behind the Bamboo Curtain about the public square singing of songs and evangelism in China. He replied, "Not many are saved at the time, but the whole church is encouraged to be more bold."

We found the same new boldness in the congregation each time we held an Alpha program or trained in prayer evangelism.

In our little church in Vancouver, we prayed our way forward into several evangelism approaches. Alpha outreach, Art in the City/ Art in the Sanctuary events, as well as a concerted effort to reach international students and new immigrants fueled our prayers and our love for our lost neighbors. Several came to Christ year by year.

We notice in the early church history, as well as in an abundance of conversions, following the pouring out of the Spirit, we experience a profusion of miracles, mighty acts of deliverance, and a torrent of spectacular healings. It would do violence to the Scripture and lessen the comprehensive reality of Christ's saving work if we did not pray eagerly and expectantly for healings, deliverance, special guidance, and other wonderful works of God. God speaks and acts with power. As long as our prayers are fueled by faith and guided by God's promises, we can be confident that if we ask, we will receive.

It is a sad reality that we have often taken our greatest struggles and turned them over to the medical and recovery professions without thought or hope that God will do His great works in answer to prayer, with or without ordinary means. We ask for God to heal someone who is sick or addicted, or pray for deliverance for one who is struggling with mental illness, but need to be renewed in bold hope that earnest and united prayer will be followed by the wonders of God through Christ.

Of course, miraculous and medical healings are not mutually exclusive. Here is a testimony of how a dear friend experienced deliverance and learned the power and purpose of prayer while in a recovery program:

> From the moment I entered treatment for alcohol and substance abuse and began to practice the Twelve Steps as a program of recovery, I realized that prayer would be a signif-

icant aspect of my desire for long-term sobriety. Once sober, I was ashamed to admit that during active addiction, my prayers were mostly selfish and one-sided. I have learned through my renewed desire to delve deeply into the gospel that constant prayer is actually the foundation of my recovery and that I must continue to pray for the salvation of others in order to fulfill God's desire for me and for His kingdom.

Kingdom prayer and looking at life through a healthier lens, while actively praying for others, has blessed me with a relationship with my Savior that I had never dreamed possible. God's authority is at the heart of my resolve to remain sober until I take my last breath.

On the other hand, works of healing and deliverance often bypass ordinary means. In the world of Islam, many thousands are introduced to Christ—Isa—through dreams and visions. God often introduces Himself to Hindus in India through healings in answer to the prayers of Christians.

God is pleased to display the splendor of His majesty and the greatness of His might. A First Nations woman from a reserve in Alberta testified, "I am a Christian for one reason. It is not by going to church. It is because Jesus has far greater power than all the other spirits. Because of His great power, I left those ways behind and became His follower."

This kind of testimony should be repeated every day in every church. God's Word taught and God's Spirit experienced in powerful ways is not a New Testament anomaly, it is normal Christianity.

Stage 3: The Spirit Forms a House of Prayer

The third stage in the Spirit's pattern for mission is the spontaneous gathering of a tightly bonded, praying community. All who long for the coming kingdom are awed (and more than a little envious) at Luke's description of the first community of believers in Acts 2:41–47 and 4:32–25:

> Those who gladly received his word were baptized . . . and they continued steadfastly in the apostles' doctrine and fellowship, in the breaking of bread, and in prayers. . . . Now all who believed were together, and had all things in common . . . breaking bread from house to house, they ate their food with gladness and simplicity of heart, praising God and having favor with all the people. And the Lord added to the church daily those who were being saved.
> ACTS 2:41–42, 44, 46–47 NKJV

The vitality and joy of the New Testament church was directly proportional to the momentum of prayer and the multiplication of new converts. A community of love and kindness formed spontaneously out of the fertile soil of evangelism. The leaders did not need to organize and promote prayer meetings; they couldn't keep people from gathering if they wanted to! In the atmosphere of radical witness, newly regenerated believers, amazing deliverance, radiant joy, contagious selflessness, and sacrificial giving sprung to life a living, multiplying community. New Christians gathered without pressure or human engineering.

It is like the formation of life itself. When DNA forms, it seems to be guided by an invisible conductor, in which amino acids and proteins join together in a synchronized dance of elements. The same is true of a praying community. Irresistibly and invisibly, the Spirit brings His people together to form the very body of Christ.

Imagine what a difference it will make today if God pours out a Spirit of prayer. Joyful and bonded gatherings will multiply spontaneously, rather than by detailed organizing and repeated exhortation. Becoming this kind of spiritually organic community fulfills the prayer and hope of every loving pastor who is fatigued by trying to gather a scattered flock.

Stage 4: New Leaders Emerge from the Growing Community

Selecting and deploying new leaders is the fourth stage in the sequence. Where there is growth, not just in numbers but in conversions and in love, new leaders always emerge. God gives leaders to His church (see Eph. 4:11). At one point, when our community was not many more than one hundred people, we held extensive leader training in prayer, teaching, and mission. Out of interest we counted those who were being trained in this way, and found we had twenty-one men and twenty-one women actively involved.

In the early church, rapid growth opened the door for new leaders. The twelve disciples were soon overwhelmed by the legitimate needs of thousands of new believers.

In the New Testament narrative, early on the opportunity to expand the leadership presented itself. Trouble arose from within the fellowship, and the Holy Spirit provided the solution. The issue was serious: widows were being neglected in the daily distribution of food. They were Grecian widows, so the implication was that Jewish leaders were being unfair to Gentile converts. Wisely, the apostles made a strategic decision. They stayed on task, expanded the leadership base, and involved the people in the process:

> The twelve summoned the full number of the disciples and said, "It is not right that we should give up preaching the word of God to serve tables. Therefore, brothers, pick out from among you seven men of good repute, full of the Spirit and of wisdom, whom we will appoint to this duty.

But we will devote ourselves to prayer and to the ministry
of the word.

ACTS 6:2–4

To the credit of the Jewish apostles, prayer remained the priority. The results were outstanding! At the same time the widows received attention and the leadership base expanded. Seven Greek believers were selected as deacons. These men became outstanding ministers, with Stephen and Philip leading the way. Rather than slowing down, the movement radically expanded. As a result, "the number of the disciples multiplied greatly in Jerusalem, and a great many of the priests became obedient to the faith" (Acts 6:7). The church was multiplied and mobilized as never before.

Stage 5: New Churches Multiply in Joy

The fruition stage of this remarkable sequence is the multiplication of new churches. Acts 9:31 reads as a summary and celebration of the first four stages: "The church throughout all Judea and Galilee and Samaria had peace and was being built up. And walking in the fear of the Lord and in the comfort of the Holy Spirit, it multiplied."

The formation of hundreds of new churches throughout Palestine marked the completion of the first phase of Christ's strategy to reach the world. The birth of new congregations fulfilled the sequence. Prayer preceded empowerment. Bold evangelism birthed new believers. Converts united in sacrificial and joyful community. The selection of new leaders mobilized the church, resulting in the formation of new congregations throughout Judea, Galilee, and Samaria. In every respect, the entire church entered, embraced, and enacted the mission of the Holy Spirit!

We have seen this happen in Canada where starting new churches is not for the timid of heart. The ground can be hard.

Yet over twelve years, from 2007–2019, a fledgling team of some eight churches, called the Grace Network, planted fourteen flourishing new works in cities across Canada, with its sights on more new endeavors.

THE HOLY SPIRIT SEQUENCE REPEATS AGAIN AND AGAIN

Each of the five stages in the Spirit's mission plan builds upon the previous one. No stage can be omitted, and the order is crucial. For example, without power through prayer, evangelism produces little fruit. Without conversion growth, community formation stalls.

This required sequence highlights a weakness in a great many mission endeavors today: an inadequate prayer base results in weak evangelistic efforts and anemic growth. Even if new churches experience numerical growth, too often it can be the result of gathering Christians who leave their previous fellowship to try out something new.[1]

The same is true for existing churches. Real Holy Spirit growth in the church begins with prayer and bold extensive evangelism. It is futile to pray for your church to grow and then ignore the clear pattern Scripture gives us.

The community will bond and grow as *there is more joy* in any church where there are new believers. New leaders will rise to the task of growing these new believers. In time, new outreach missions will fan out from this radiant core.

Not only do the five stages build upon one another, but so too must the sequence be continually repeated. This is how the Holy Spirit works. The five stages that initially occurred at Pentecost repeated in striking detail in Acts 4.

After the first wave of advance, the stage was set for a cosmic collision between the church and the very rulers that conspired the death of Christ. The young church had experienced explosive growth. Thousands were coming to Christ, and in so doing were discovering community, healing, and joy. The political and religious powers were alarmed; they realized the movement of Christ was not going to fade away. So they arrested Peter and John.

The enemy hit back hard. The religious rulers could not accept that the disciples were preaching a crucified and risen Christ and were performing miracles just as He had. They demanded of Peter and John, "By what power or by what name did you do this?" (Acts 4:7). When they realized that the name and power in question was none other than the same Jesus they crucified, they sharpened their assault: "They conferred with one another, saying . . . 'In order that it may spread no further among the people, let us warn them to speak no more to anyone in this name.' So they called them and charged them not to speak or teach at all in the name of Jesus" (4:15–18).

The response of the church to these threats was telling. Leaders and people went to prayer—but not just any prayer. This was concerted, united, kingdom prayer. They cried out to the King of kings to advance His kingdom:

> When they heard it, they lifted their voices together to God and said, "Sovereign Lord, who made the heaven and the earth and the sea and everything in them, who through the mouth of our father David, your servant, said by the Holy Spirit,
>
> > 'Why did the Gentiles rage,
> >   and the peoples plot in vain?
> > The kings of the earth set themselves,
> >   and the rulers were gathered together,
> >   against the Lord and against his Anointed'—

for truly in this city there were gathered together against your holy servant Jesus, whom you anointed, both Herod and Pontius Pilate, along with the Gentiles and the peoples of Israel, to do whatever your hand and your plan had predestined to take place. And now, Lord, look upon their threats and grant to your servants to continue to speak your word with all boldness, while you stretch out your hand to heal, and signs and wonders are performed through the name of your holy servant Jesus."

ACTS 4:24–30

What follows is, event by event, phrase by phrase, clearly a repetition of the sequence in chapters 1 and 2:

When they had prayed, the place in which they were gathered together was shaken [Stage 1], and they were all filled with the Holy Spirit and continued to speak the word of God with boldness [Stage 2].

Now the full number of those who believed were of one heart and soul, and no one said that any of the things that belonged to him was his own, but they had everything in common [Stage 3]. And with great power the apostles were giving their testimony to the resurrection of the Lord Jesus, and great grace was upon them all. There was not a needy person among them, for as many as were owners of lands or houses sold them and brought the proceeds of what was sold.

ACTS 4:31–34

Once again, power fell from on high. This time the earth quaked. All the believers were filled with the Spirit (again!), resulting in bold evangelism by leaders and people. The community was further strengthened in love, prayer, and good works. Leader mobilization [Stage 4] and church planting [Stage 5] soon followed.

This repetition of the sequence encourages us to cry out for the Holy Spirit again and again. This earthquake reveals that Pentecost is the epicenter of many empowerments for the church for that day and ours. The pouring out of the Spirit is not a one-time event, nor are the spectacular manifestations of Christ's power only for that day.

In an abbreviated way, this prayer sequence is repeated another six times in Acts. Every advance began with prayer, bold witness followed, and the fellowship grew in numbers and strength.

In Acts 6:1–7, the leaders resolved to devote themselves to prayer and the Word. Following this prayer resolve, the leadership base expanded, the fellowship strengthened, and conversions multiplied.

In Acts 7:60, 8:4, and 11:21, widespread evangelism took place after Stephen's prayer. He echoed the prayer of his Savior who forgave His tormentors: "Lord, do not hold this sin against them." He was rewarded with a glorious vision of Jesus. Soon a host of lay evangelists became the first apostolic witnesses to the Gentile world! Scattered out from Jerusalem, they went to Antioch and led non-Jews to Christ.

In Acts 10, Peter and Cornelius' prayers preceded the gospel going to the Gentile world. They prayed about different things at different times and in different situations. Though they both were unaware, they were having a prayer meeting that the Holy Spirit used to break the barrier between Jew and Gentile. Cornelius and his entire household were converted and filled with the Holy Spirit. The leaders of the whole church were mobilized to move ahead with the Spirit's plans to reach the world for Christ.

In Acts 12:5 and 12, an all-night prayer meeting brought deliverance for Peter, who was in jail, frustrated the enemies of the church, and opened the gate of the city "of its own accord."

Acts 13:1–4 highlights how the prophets of Antioch prayed their way into the global mission. While they were praying and ministering to God, the Holy Spirit took charge. Their little plans met the great plans of Christ: "Set apart for me Barnabas and Saul for the work to which I have called them" (v. 2). There is an important lesson here: the Holy Spirit reveals His mission strategies as we pray. Apart from prayer, the specific plans of the Holy Spirit remain hidden.

Finally, in Acts 16, Paul and Barnabas were imprisoned in Philippi. As they worshiped and prayed, they experienced another mighty earthquake, the prison doors opened, and the jailer and his household were saved. There would soon be a church family in Philippi.

THE SEQUENCE REPEATS TODAY

Luke's narration of the repeated sequence is no coincidence. It is an organic blend of the Spirit and prayer. In fact, it is a message from Christ to His church. The sequence of prayer empowerment, bold mission enactment, community formation, leader multiplication, and new church creation will be repeated again and again across the ages.

An enhanced illustration of the five stages of kingdom-advance looks like this:

EVANGELISTIC ADVANCE

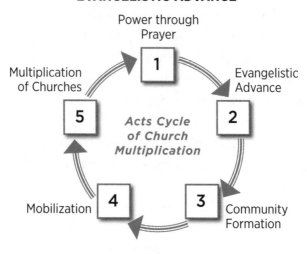

The implication is clear and convicting for us today. To make progress we need to start from the beginning. Leaders need to lead from the knees. God's people need to gather in prayer. We all need to cry out for God to forgive all prayerlessness and to ask for the Holy Spirit to initiate the sequence once again!

Kingdom-Come Prayer Today

1. What was new to you about this sequence of Holy Spirit mission? Why is it so important? What is the result of going out of sequence?

2. What does waiting in prayer mean to you? Do you find it hard to wait in prayer? Why?

3. Considering your church or ministry, what is the balance across each stage of Holy Spirit advance? In what ways can you keep prayer a priority in each of the five stages?

6

HOW PRAYER FUELS A GLOBAL MOVEMENT

The prayer life of the apostle Paul transforms the world

Paul the apostle was no armchair quarterback. He led his team from the field of battle. He called his plays in the face of fierce opposition. He didn't form his strategies within the safe, cloistered walls of the study but from the frontlines of mission.

While journeying from city to city on Roman roads, Paul wrote his letters to those he had ushered into the kingdom. He engaged the world head on and built a team to do the same. Because he led from the battlefront, people listened to him. His teaching was filled with a relevant immediacy. His prayers were filled

> **From his fourteen epistles, we encounter a staggering number of prayers, prayer requests, and exhortations to pray. Paul prayed sixty-five times and referred to prayer another twenty-two times in his letters.**

with love for the church and burden for the lost world.

In the same way, whenever our hearts are moved to pray for Christ's church and her global mission, we move from being spectators to being participants, from the bleachers to the field of play.

HOW PAUL FUELED HIS MISSION THROUGH PRAYER

Paul tells us the kingdom of God is about power (see 1 Cor. 4:20). Prayer empowers gospel ministry. Paul had a ministry of power because he ministered in prayer. He left no doubt about the priority of prayer in his life and mission: from his fourteen epistles, we encounter a staggering number of prayers, prayer requests, and exhortations to pray. Paul prayed sixty-five times and referred to prayer another twenty-two times in his letters. This includes forty-five benediction and doxology prayers, along with twenty prayers of blessing. In addition, he wrote eleven encouragements to pray, four teachings on how to pray, and seven prayer requests. In five places, with thanksgiving, Paul narrated answers to prayer. We think of Paul as a great theologian, but we also have to acknowledge him equally to be a mighty man of prayer.

Once we discover the sheer volume of prayer concentration in the life and ministry of Paul, we need no further proof that prayer is at the heart of every effective endeavor to expand Christ's church.

Paul's specific prayers, infused with gospel theology, permeate his letters. For example, throughout the book of Ephesians, we find five prayers of blessing (benedictions), two extensive prayers, two exhortations to pray, and one prayer request.

It is a poor study of Paul's letters to consider his teaching and neglect his prayer life, for Paul ministered as much by prayer as by doctrine. There is interplay of prayer and teaching in all of Paul's letters. For example, scattered throughout the brief letters of 1 and 2 Thessalonians are nine prayers of benediction, six intercessory prayers, one exhortation to pray, and two prayer requests. Once we discover the sheer volume of prayer concentration in the life and ministry of Paul, we need no further proof that prayer is at the heart of every effective endeavor to expand Christ's church.

Paul's prayer life is a living motivation for every believer—especially those involved in apostolic work, evangelists, missionaries, and campus workers.

Let's look at the types of prayers Paul prayed so we can get a better sense of his passion for the church and how his prayers fueled a global ministry revolution.

Benediction and Doxology Prayers

In the more than forty benediction and doxology prayers, Paul both pronounced and invoked God's blessing. We find most of these prayers at the beginning and end of his letters. It is a mistake, however, to skip over them as mere conventions of greeting and salutation. These blessings are rich with the life of the Spirit and are able to impart the very life of Christ. Paul was fulfilling the priestly calling of all believers, the calling that began with Aaron: "Aaron was set apart . . . that he . . . should . . . minister to [the LORD] and pronounce blessings in his name forever" (1 Chron. 23:13).

Here are some examples of Paul's benediction prayers:

> May the God of endurance and encouragement grant you to live in such harmony with one another, in accord with Christ Jesus, that together you may with one voice glorify the God and Father of our Lord Jesus Christ.
>
> ROMANS 15:5–6

May the God of hope fill you with all joy and peace in believing, so that by the power of the Holy Spirit you may abound in hope.

ROMANS 15:13

The grace of the Lord Jesus Christ and the love of God and the fellowship of the Holy Spirit be with you all.

2 CORINTHIANS 13:14

May the Lord make you increase and abound in love for one another and for all, as we do for you, so that he may establish your hearts blameless in holiness before our God and Father, at the coming of our Lord Jesus with all his saints.

1 THESSALONIANS 3:12–13

Now may the God of peace himself sanctify you completely, and may your whole spirit and soul and body be kept blameless at the coming of our Lord Jesus Christ. He who calls you is faithful; he will surely do it.

1 THESSALONIANS 5:23–24

These invocations and benedictions were not mere wishes. The word of prayer has the power to impart the blessing prayed for. As Paul's readers heard and received these words by faith, they were filled with the Holy Spirit's power and blessing.

Surveying the heft of these prayers, we realize how much richer our prayer lives would be—and how much more effective our ministry to others—if we filled our prayers with these priestly pronouncements.

Paul's Prayers Impart Blessing

Paul's writings include twenty other prayers for the churches. Consider Ephesians, in which prayer radiates throughout the letter. These are not polite one-sentence invocations but instead entire paragraphs devoted to intercession. Two all-encompassing, "monster prayers" in chapters 1 and 3 contain some of the richest doctrine in all of Scripture:

> I [pray] . . . that the God of our Lord Jesus Christ, the Father of glory, may give you the Spirit of wisdom and of revelation in the knowledge of him, having the eyes of your hearts enlightened, that you may know what is the hope to which he has called you, what are the riches of his glorious inheritance in the saints, and what is the immeasurable greatness of his power toward us who believe, according to the working of his great might that he worked in Christ when he raised him from the dead and seated him at his right hand in the heavenly places.
>
> EPHESIANS 1:16–20

Wisdom, revelation, knowledge, and *enlightenment.* All the words of Greek and Roman philosophy are included in a single prayer—even in a single clause of a larger prayer!

What a treasure is ours through prayer! How great is the contrast between Christian spirituality and all others. Surely there is more spiritual substance and heavenly riches in this one verse of prayer than in all the teachings of Deepak Chopra, Dalai Lama, and Eckhart Tolle combined! Yet Paul was not being philosophical. He was being pastoral and intentional, confident his prayer would impart these supernatural realities to the church.

Today's false prophets offer peace through yogic meditations and mantras. They say, "Your soul's needs will be fulfilled by right breathing, right words, and right postures. The key to happiness is living in the present, the everlasting 'now.'" For them, true happiness depends upon a subjective detachment from the storms of life and the ceaseless cultivation of mindfulness.

By contrast, a Christian is concerned not with "living in the present" but in "living in the Presence." The outcome of this God-orientation is a radical and courageous engagement with the world, not detachment from the storms of life. Through prayer, the peace of God so overwhelms a believer's soul that he or she is able to rise above the chaos of life and is filled with power to dive into the work of restoring fractured lives in a broken world.

A believer has an entirely different experience of spiritual power and happiness. There is no comparison between the peace that comes from the fortress of God's mighty presence and the peace of inconstant awareness and emotions. Reread the above prayer and you cannot miss the striking difference between Christian and neo-pagan spirituality. A believer's daily security rests on the rock-solid foundation of Christ, not on an inner state. Through simple prayer, Christians experience an objective peace rooted in the power of God and the accomplished reality of Christ's resurrection. The peace won through prayer is not self-contained but spreads like salt and leaven.

Consider what is happening today in the world of Islam. Since 1993 more and more Christians (now many thousands) have been praying through the thirty days of Ramadan for God to visit and bless Muslims with a knowledge of Jesus Christ. Since then, researchers are finding that the tide of resistance is reversing and that countless thousands, even millions, of Muslims are becoming followers of Jesus.[1]

As men and women of peace unite to pray Christ-rich prayers, blessings of the kingdom multiply, and peace with God and reconciliation between people begins to spread throughout the entire world.

Prayer Encouragements and Instructions

In his letters, Paul added eleven exhortations and four instructions for Christians to pray. Consider this practical encouragement to the Philippian believers:

> Rejoice in the Lord always; again I will say, rejoice. Let your reasonableness be known to everyone. The Lord is at hand; do not be anxious about anything, but in everything by prayer and supplication with thanksgiving let your requests be made known to God. And the peace of God, which surpasses all understanding, will guard your hearts and your minds in Christ Jesus.
> **PHILIPPIANS 4:4-7**

Paul pastored the people by encouraging them to take all their sorrows and trials to God in prayer. Paul took from his own experiences of answered prayer in difficult, even desperate, times and passed it on.

Good leaders realize that their best shepherding often happens as they pray with others under their care. Hours of advice and counsel are often transcended in a single prayer. God gives wisdom and enlightenment. Prayer brings God into the conversation.

Paul's Personal Prayer Requests

Paul not only prayed for the churches, he asked for personal prayers seven times. Paul fueled his mission to the Gentile world with the prayers of the very churches he helped plant.

In his prayer requests, Paul's focus was apostolic and missionary.

He asked supporting churches to pray for three things: greater boldness, greater opportunities, and great deliverance:

> Pray also for me, that whenever I speak, words may be given me so that I will fearlessly make known the mystery of the gospel, for which I am an ambassador in chains. Pray that I may declare it fearlessly, as I should.
> EPHESIANS 6:19–20 NIV

> Continue steadfastly in prayer . . . pray also for us, that God may open to us a door for the word . . . that I may make it clear, which is how I ought to speak.
> COLOSSIANS 4:2–4

> He delivered us from such a deadly peril, and he will deliver us. On him we have set our hope that he will deliver us again. You also must help us by prayer, so that many will give thanks on our behalf for the blessing granted us through the prayers of many.
> 2 CORINTHIANS 1:10–11

Notice the object of these requests. Paul asked prayer for himself, but not so much for the lost he sought to reach as for his own effectiveness. This is strategic. Paul had been given the promises. He was the instrument; he knew God could change and empower him. Effective missionary praying begins with praying for the messenger.

It was true then, and it is true today: if you want to reach a world, ask others to pray for you. You can assume that little lasting fruit happens in you or through you without faithful prayer support. Also note, when these prayers were answered, it was vitally important to give thanks to God and also to share answers with those who prayed (see 2 Cor. 1:18, Phil. 1:18–22).

No one is strong enough on their own to enter apostolic mission of evangelism. Paul met storm and fury from evil men and evil spirits as he went about proclaiming the Good News. While working with mission leaders for more than thirty years, the first thing I do is exhort a new planter, campus worker, or missionary to recruit one hundred people of prayer to pray for them each week until a prayer base is established in the new church or mission—and then I exhort them to ask the same one hundred to continue to pray as the mission matures. The first thing this prayer team asks on behalf of the leader and mission are the protection and power of the Holy Spirit and for a deeper gospel awareness of the presence of Christ. Prayers for boldness, open doors, and deliverance follow.

MISSION IMPLICATIONS OF PAUL'S PRAYER REQUESTS

As we study Paul's prayer requests, we can see three mission implications they had for the global movement, which also apply to how we pray.

First, like Paul, we need always to pray for boldness to share the gospel. God will hear these prayers and give us the courage to lead others to Christ. The implication of Paul's requests is clear. Without prayer, fear rules our hearts. Nothing is more daunting in the Christian life than evangelism. Jesus warned that it is the very nature of the world to be at enmity with God and with His servants. (John 15:18–25 is a sober reminder.) You confess you are afraid to proclaim the gospel? You should be. Paul knew fear too! Yet no one could question his resolve to bring Christ into every conversation. The road from fear to freedom is traversed by prayer, especially as others unite in prayer on our behalf.

So when the gathered believers heard the leaders warn them not to preach about Jesus, they raised their voice to God with one accord and said:

"Lord, You are God. . . . Now, Lord, look on their threats, and grant to Your servants that with all boldness they may speak Your word." . . .

And when they had prayed, the place where they were assembled together was shaken; and they were all filled with the Holy Spirit, and they spoke the Word of God with boldness.

ACTS 4:24, 29, 31 NKJV

As someone has noted, "The devil trembles when he sees God's weakest child on his knees." As one missionary friend in a persecuted country put it, "When we pray like the early Christians did, we move from an invaded people to an invading army."

The second mission implication we need to understand is that Paul prayed for open doors. This is significant. This means that the doors to a city, town, village—and even the heart of a friend—remain closed until opened by prayer. The good news is that the gate of the city opens "of its own accord" after the earnest and united prayer of God's people (see Acts 12:5, 10). Like Paul, we can expect great results when we pray with others for open doors. Let's look at two occasions Paul prayed this way:

I will stay in Ephesus . . . for a wide door for effective work has opened to me, and there are many adversaries.

1 CORINTHIANS 16:8–9

When I came to Troas to preach the gospel of Christ . . . a door was opened for me in the Lord. . . . But thanks be to God, who in Christ always leads us in triumphal procession, and through us spreads the fragrance of the knowledge of him everywhere.

2 CORINTHIANS 2:12, 14

A third mission implication is that we will encounter opposition whenever and wherever we preach the gospel. Like Paul, we need to pray to be delivered from evil people and evil demons. As we pray, God will deliver us!

Here is one of Paul's answers to praying for deliverance:

> The Lord stood by me and strengthened me, so that through me the message might be fully proclaimed and all the Gentiles might hear it. So I was rescued from the lion's mouth. The Lord will rescue me from every evil deed and bring me safely into his heavenly kingdom. To him be the glory forever and ever. Amen.
>
> **2 TIMOTHY 4:17–18**

At present, there is an increasing urgency to pray for deliverance from those who oppose the gospel. Around the world, more and more believers are being imprisoned and martyred even today. Open Doors, a mission organization that supports persecuted Christians throughout the world, reports that Christians are the most persecuted group in the world, calling it "one of the biggest human rights issues of the era."[2] As evidence, they cite the 2019 World Watch List, which reported that in the period between November 1, 2017, and October 31, 2018, the following took place globally:

- More than 245 million Christians live in places where they experience high levels of persecution.
- 4,305 Christians were killed for their faith.
- 1,847 churches and other Christian buildings were attacked.
- 3,150 believers were detained without trial, arrested, sentenced, or imprisoned.[3]

Also, a report recently commissioned by Great Britain's foreign secretary, Jeremy Hunt, indicates that in parts of the world, persecution of Christians has nearly reached genocide levels.[4]

A prayer for deliverance is not a nicety—it is a necessity. To make this point in a darkly humorous way, an exchange between two believers has surfaced from a country that is hostile to the gospel. In this country, Christians experience great persecution, and many have become martyrs. The exchange goes like this:

> You say you are being investigated. Be glad you were not interrogated.
> You say you were interrogated. Be glad you were not arrested.
> You say you were arrested. Be glad you were not tortured.
> You say you were tortured. Be glad you were not killed.
> You say you were killed. Be glad! You are in heaven!

Jesus told a stern parable referring to visiting our brothers and sisters imprisoned for their faith:

> The King will say to those on his right, "Come, you who are blessed by my Father, inherit the kingdom prepared for you . . . I was in prison and you came to me." . . .
> Then he will say to those on his left, "Depart from me, you cursed, into the eternal fire prepared for the devil and his angels. For I was . . . sick and in prison and you did not visit me."
> MATTHEW 25:34, 36, 41–43

Though we may not be able to visit those being imprisoned for their faith, we can bless them in prayer. We can be with them as we pray, because we are with the One who is with them when we intercede for their comfort, endurance, and deliverance.

Consider when Peter was imprisoned by Herod. Fellow believers not only loved their leader, but their empathy was doubled because it was Passover, a time when Israel was to remember their bondage in Egypt. Though the gathered Christians were not able to visit Peter face to face, in solidarity they blessed him in prayer through the night (see Acts 12:5, 12). Their prayers were heard, and just as the Israelites were freed from Egypt on the night of the Passover, Peter was freed from his prison. The gospel message greatly multiplied and Herod the persecutor was struck down by an angel of the Lord.

What mighty acts of God might the persecuted Christians experience if all God's people lifted up a common cry for their deliverance?

LEARNING TO PRAY AS PAUL PRAYED

By examining Paul's prayers we can understand his laser-like focus on blessing. By praying as he prayed, we experience and impart these blessings of holiness, love, and courage. We are a priesthood of believers. When we lift holy hands in intercession, we become like the Old Testament priests who were appointed to bless the people (see 1 Chron. 23:13). We become like Jesus, who ever lives to intercede (Heb. 7:25).

There are a number of ways we can pray as the apostle prayed:

Be Faithful to Pray for Other Believers

"I thank God whom I serve, as did my ancestors, with a clear conscience, as I remember you constantly in my prayers night and day" (2 Tim. 1:3).

Give Thanks for Your Brothers and Sisters

"First, I thank my God through Jesus Christ for all of you, because your faith is being reported all over the world" (Rom. 1:8 NIV).

"I thank my God every time I remember you. In all my prayers for all of you, I always pray with joy because of your partnership in the gospel from the first day until now" (Phil. 1:3–5 NIV).

"We give thanks to God always for all of you, constantly mentioning you in our prayers, remembering before our God and Father your work of faith and labor of love and steadfastness of hope in our Lord Jesus Christ" (1 Thess. 1:2–3).

Ask for Grace and Holiness to Abound in the Church

"[We pray this so that you may] walk in a manner worthy of the Lord, fully pleasing to him: bearing fruit in every good work and increasing in the knowledge of God" (Col. 1:10).

"May he strengthen your hearts so that you will be blameless and holy in the presence of our God and Father when our Lord Jesus comes with all his holy ones" (1 Thess. 3:13 NIV).

Pray that Love for One Another May Increase

"[I pray that you] know the love of Christ that surpasses knowledge, that you may be filled with all the fullness of God" (Eph. 3:19).

"This is my prayer: that your love may abound more and more in knowledge and depth of insight" (Phil. 1:9 NIV).

Ask God for Believers to Become Rich and Effective in Spiritual Knowledge

"I keep asking that the God of our Lord Jesus Christ, the glorious Father, may give you the Spirit of wisdom and revelation" (Eph. 1:17 NIV).

"I pray that the sharing of your faith may become effective for the full knowledge of every good thing that is in us for the sake of Christ" (Philem. 6).

Pray for God's People to Be Filled with the Presence and Power of Christ

"I pray that the eyes of your heart may be enlightened in order that you may know . . . his incomparably great power for us who believe. That power is the same as the mighty strength he exerted when he raised Christ from the dead and seated him at his right hand in the heavenly realms" (Eph. 1:18–20 NIV).

"[We pray this in order that you] walk in a manner worthy of the Lord, fully pleasing to him: bearing fruit in every good work and increasing in the knowledge of God; being strengthened with all power, according to his glorious might, for all endurance and patience with joy" (Col. 1:10–11).

CHURCH TRANSFORMATION THROUGH BLESSING PRAYER

Imagine if our prayers were filled with blessings like these prayers of Paul! We would stop judging each other. We would cease giving advice or attempting to fix others. We wouldn't close our eyes to the sins and failings of others, but we would pray for fresh convictions flowing from the fullness of Christ's Spirit.

Paul was aware of the serious problems and sins in the churches, but that didn't prevent him from pronouncing benedictions upon them. Benediction prayers are transformative—starting with the one who is praying them. As we pray this way, our tendency to be critical will weaken, and our affection and concern for others will expand.

There is great hope here for Christian leadership. Once we begin to follow Paul's example and spend much of our prayer time blessing the church as he did, we are already fueling the movement of God with heaven's encouragement. As we pray the blessings of Scripture for one another, God will surely answer and we will behold the evidence of transformed lives. As the courage and love atmosphere heats up, blessing one another in prayer will become contagious, and others will stream to join in. Yes, for many, there will need to be a radical realignment of our prayer lives. It will take patience and perseverance—but the rewards of kingdom advance will be infinitely worth it.

In studying Paul's letters, we see the one overarching mandate for anyone who desires to be a godly leader or make a long-term spiritual impact: to be a minister of the Word, we must minister in prayer. Prayer complements and completes the teaching. Just as prayer apart from the Word lacks its true aim, the Word apart from prayer lacks its intended power.

The authority of Word and prayer working together is the key to mission advance. As an effective leader, Paul ministered as much by prayer as by teaching. For the apostle, prayer completed the teaching. Paul turned to prayer again and again to tend the sheep and to advance the gospel. What teaching cannot accomplish, prayer can.

It is not hard to start praying like Paul. You can pray the very prayers he prayed. I have memorized several of them so I can easily bring them to mind at any time. Remember, Paul's prayers not only contain the words of God, these prayers *are* the Word of God! When we ask according to God's will, He gives what we ask for (see 1 John 5:14). To pray the words of God is to pray the will of God.

Paul's prayers were like the fusion core that fuels the expansive radiance of the sun. Ours can be too.

Kingdom-Come Prayer Today

1. Review some of your own prayers. How much of your time and focus do you spend praying for God to bless His church?

2. The next time you meet with your group, pray for each other by name for spiritual blessing and growth, for courage in personal spiritual warfare, and for deliverance from evil in the ongoing battle.

3. Pray for leaders in your church—for increasing boldness, for open doors of opportunity, and for spiritual protection and deliverance.

HOW PRAYER BRINGS URBAN RENEWAL

The seeds of kingdom building are planted by a praying church

The kingdom of Christ advances in both abrupt and gradual ways. Regardless of the pace, the result is a world turned upside down.

In Old Testament revivals, in the life of Jesus, at Pentecost, throughout the early period of the church, and in all the Pentecost aftershocks reverberating throughout history to awaken spiritual revival, the kingdom comes suddenly, unexpectedly, and in manifest power. Thus, in Acts, the kingdom arrives and advances in wind, fire, and earthquake (see Acts 2 and 4); prison doors give way to miraculous release (Acts 12:6–7; 16:26); a city gate opens "of its own accord" (Acts 12:10); and citizens are stirred either to great joy or an angry frenzy (see point 5 below). Behind each tectonic upheaval lies the earnest and united prayers of God's people.

In times between revivals, less visible but equally profound kingdom harvest proceeds wherever Christ is proclaimed and obeyed. The roots of faith's tiny "mustard seed" grow unnoticed until a rich forest of faith sprouts, spreads, and shelters many under its canopy. Whenever many are saved by prayer-fueled evangelism, repercussions of social justice, mercy, and repentance spread throughout the land.

Likewise, using another of Jesus' metaphors, after the salt is added, it penetrates the entire offering with preserving and enhancing properties. Still again, once leaven is added, though it starts small, over time the yeast eventually leavens the whole. Mustard seed, salt, and leaven are metaphors Jesus used to illustrate the steady, formidable advance of the kingdom throughout the ages until "this gospel of the kingdom will be proclaimed throughout the whole world" (Matt. 24:14) and "till he has established justice in the earth" (Isa. 42:4). God rebuilds church and city through the prayers, proclamation, and good works of His church.

Whenever the church is losing influence in the surrounding culture, the problem lies with the church, not the culture.

From first tremors of spiritual conversions and renewal, leaven and salt of the kingdom start working their way into the culture. This is critically important, for whenever the church is losing influence in the surrounding culture, the problem lies with the church, not the culture. As Jesus warned, if the salt can lose its saltiness, it no longer serves any purpose (see Matt. 5:13). In our time and place, though we see noble ministries of mercy and faithful churches that have held the fort, many Christians have drifted away from lives of kingdom prayer, bold evangelism, and social justice. As a result the church weakens, and the surrounding culture pushes and bullies the church and its saving message to the sidelines. To progress, we must start over.

Hope is not far off. Wherever the Good News is sown, the seed begins to grow. When we started Grace Vancouver Church, our intent was two-fold. First, we would pray and build a praying church. Second, we would ask God to insert us into the heart and artery of the city. As Randy Nabors, a visionary colleague who for many years served as an inner-city pastor, put it, "Your church should be so indispensable to the community that if you were to leave, it would tear the heart out of it."[1]

Over the following years, God answered our prayers and opened doors. Even though our church was never more than two hundred people, it was filled with willing servants. For instance, thanks to the initiative of one of our younger women, we partnered with a community center and a Catholic church in a nearby area to start Showers for the Shelterless. We provided to the homeless in the community something most of us take for granted—a daily shower. They could park their cart, leave their pet dogs while someone watched them, and receive a hot shower, rich hospitality, a hot breakfast, gallons of coffee, a newspaper, a haircut, and even some new socks or gloves.

Another gifted leader in our church community gathered the artists and worship team leaders to create a flourishing ministry called Art in the City, Art in the Sanctuary. Twice a year hundreds of friends and neighbors crowded our building on weekend nights to enjoy the work of all area artists, not just those who were part of our church. Our arts team would choose a theme, and we invited artists to submit paintings, prints, and sculptures that fit the theme. After a rich interplay of city and sanctuary, we invited people to come on Sunday morning to hear a sermon about God, creativity, and the arts.

From small beginnings, the leaven was working. All because

we started with prayer and a willingness for God to use us.

God has a plan and He will provide the gifts and leaders if we wait on Him to lead. Urban renewal begins in small and unnoticed ways, taking time for the leaven of the gospel to do its work. Jesus tells us the yeast of the kingdom remains hidden until it penetrates the whole (see Luke 13:20–21). And it penetrates directly through and because of our prayers.

SOCIETAL CHANGES BEGIN WITHIN

Jesus' use of simple metaphors like seed, salt, and leaven highlights the revolutionary new order of the new covenant. Revival in the Old Testament kingdom era involved visible outward changes that quickly filtered down to the entire culture. For example, after public prayers of repentance, kings removed idols, tore down places of idol worship, and killed false prophets. Immediately public leaders restored legitimate temple service and approved priests, leaders, and liturgy. Righteous and repentant kings instilled judicial and military changes as well.

In the New Testament, however, spiritual renewal began within people's hearts. The first objective is the renewal of souls, and the means are the sword of the Word and acts of love and kindness. As hymn writer Ernest Shurtleff so aptly described:

> *Not with swords' loud clashing*
> *or roll of stirring drums;*
> *with deeds of love and mercy*
> *the heavenly kingdom comes.*[2]

As they pursued that change, the New Testament community planted seeds that eventually reshaped the world in the following ways:

1. The Early Church Is a Community of Equals

Following the events of Pentecost, the mustard seed of the gospel spread through every facet of society, providing a far-reaching network of branches to sustain social and spiritual renewal for every kind of people. Unlike the existing Jewish socio-religious construct with its centralized government and heredity-based religious class, the newly born church opened its doors to all believers, a remarkable example of a populist movement: "Here there is not Greek and Jew, circumcised and uncircumcised, barbarian, Scythian, slave, free; but Christ is all, and in all" (Col. 3:11).

The powers that be take note: the leaders of this Christ movement were "common men" with no formal training, no pedigree, or education (Acts 4:13), and the community of believers was open to all. Anyone could join the early church, enjoy all its privileges, and even become a prophet or leader. Leaders and people met together in a common fellowship of prayer, Scripture, and sacrament (Acts 2:42–47). With this kind of non-discriminating and overflowing hospitality, it was no wonder these Christ followers found "favor with all the people."

The practice of openness, shared fellowship, and communal helpfulness inspired onlookers to overcome the fear of persecution and join the young church. The early church both repelled and attracted those outside. Despite the fact that joining was a risky proposition, this sharing, loving community proved irresistible: "None of the rest dared join them, but the people held them in high esteem. And more than ever believers were added to the Lord, multitudes of both men and women" (Acts 5:13–14).

We need to examine the current "attractional-church" model to be sure we have a balance between the two dynamic forces of our church communities. Every true church will repel some and attract others.

2. Holding Property in Common Defines Generosity for Future Generations

While the first believers had a right to own things, they chose to give much of it away. Mandated giving was part of the social compact of God's people from their earliest Law-receiving days, but this new practice was a departure from the law of tithing. It was wholly voluntary, representing a new Spirit-led construct of selflessness. Sacrificial generosity ushered in a social and spiritual revolution of world-changing proportions: "All who believed were together and had all things in common. And they were selling their possessions and belongings and distributing the proceeds to all, as any had need" (Acts 2:44–45).

The best times in any people's history are the periods of human generosity, when the poor are embraced and provided for. In Israel according to God's law, one year in every fifty was called the Year of Jubilee. Throughout the land, all property was to be returned without cost to the original owner. Years of Jubilee were intended to create a rich culture of compassion, restoration, and justice. Tragically, we have no record that the Old Covenant people obeyed this practice.

In the early church, however, new believers had been set free from their debts to God. Acting without compulsion they exhibited a new attitude toward their possessions. The principles of Old Testament-mandated Jubilee were spontaneously enacted; property was restored to everyday people, without directive or law (see Acts 2:44–45 and 4:32). While this revolutionary practice of extravagant charity began with the church, the practice of shared property acts as leaven in every civilization captured by the gospel.

The more Christianity influences a people or society, the greater the generosity and charity. Wherever the gospel of Christ is preached and received, the result is that new churches, hospitals, missions, schools, and other ministries of kindness are established. This multiplying of institutions for the common good leads to a flourishing society.

3. The Early Church Set the Pattern for Representative Government

The early church practiced a unique form of representative democracy in which people chose their own leaders. Eventually, centuries later, this seed grew and reshaped statecraft in countries throughout the world.

The episode we find in Acts 6 manifests the enfranchising of common believers, the "liberation of the laity," and the strategic expansion of leadership. Beyond the twelve apostles, leaders elected and appointed others from among them "known to be full of the Spirit and wisdom" (v. 3 NIV) to provide the care and oversight of the kingdom community:

> This proposal pleased the whole group. They chose Stephen, a man full of faith and of the Holy Spirit; also Philip, Procorus, Nicanor, Timon, Parmenas, and Nicolas from Antioch, a convert to Judaism. They presented these men to the apostles, who prayed and laid their hands on them.
>
> ACTS 6:5–6 NIV

This practice of choosing "from among you" (v. 3) represented a momentous governmental shift from a fixed and hereditary hierarchy of the Old Testament order to a representative democracy. God's people, for the first time, chose their leaders from their own number, and these new leaders were empowered to act. The unique aspect of biblical democracy, in contrast with Athenian elections for example, was that church leaders were called not only to act on behalf of the people who voted for them but first of all to represent God before the people.

Following this revolution was the conversion of "a great many of the priests" (v. 7). Priests were at the heart of that society, so their turning to Christ could not fail to sow seeds for radical change. It is hardly speculative to imagine these leaders deeply affected by this new form of governance. Perhaps they had grown fatigued under the religious hierarchy. Regardless, they were hungry for a new order—and found it in the early church.

If we are honest, we have not followed the early church's example. Many churches have a leader-centered, top-down model, where clergy and ordained leaders carry out key decisions and essential ministries. This sets a ceiling in a church, hindering the multiplication of new leaders. This is one reason why God's people become spectators and mere churchgoers. Too often, ordained leaders have been slow to allow everyday believers to share in decision-making and training them to assume key places of leadership and disciple making. How refreshingly different it would be, and how quickly the leadership base would multiply, if we followed the cue of these early Christians.

4. The First Pentecost Redefined Race and Tribe

The first Pentecost signaled a common humanity, as Jews from every nation heard the praises of God in their own language. Another kind of Pentecost happened a few years later in Antioch when this city became the epicenter not only of evangelistic advance but also of radical interethnic transformation and community formation. The first "tongues of fire" on the heads of the 120 Jews spread rapidly beyond Palestine. Burning away the old barriers of tribe and language made way for a new multiethnic expression of the people of God and the flames of revival sweep ever outward into the Gentile world.

As things ignited in Antioch of Syria, the church experienced the typical effect of gospel advance: a great many turned to the Lord. However, another brief but world-changing phrase was added this time, and in Antioch, "the disciples were first called Christians" (Acts 11:26).

This new word for disciples of Jesus heralded the beginning of a global revolution! Antioch was a walled city—not only on the perimeter but also within its outer walls—populated by a multi-ethnic mix of Syrians, Greeks, Romans, and Jews, with each tribe occupying its own walled quarter.

As the disciples multiplied greatly in Antioch, they began to meet frequently. The result was the formation of a multiethnic Christian community of Syrians, Greeks, Romans, and Jews. Up to now, primary loyalty and identity had been connected with individual tribes ("Paul, a Jew from Tarsus," for example). But these disciples received a new identity by a new King, and the result was a new kind of deep and permanent communion with one another that transcended their tribe. The only way for the rest of the city to identify this never-before-imagined multi-tiethnic, radically bonded community was to give them a new name—*Christians*.

Jesus promised that His church would be a city set on a hill (see Matt. 5:14). The Christians in Antioch were fulfilling this word of Christ—in effect, Christians became a city within the city, and the world would never be the same.

Today, one sign that the Holy Spirit is igniting the gospel in cities around the world is the blending and bonding of Christians from various ethnic backgrounds. The Good News melts away racism and tribalism, refuting the principle that "like should gather with like." Churches are changing from monochromatic to kaleidoscopic.

5. Gospel Encounters Altered the Existing Religious and Social Order

When Philip preached the gospel in Samaria, God granted a dramatic display of Holy Spirit power: "Unclean spirits, crying out with a loud voice, came out of many who had them, and many who were paralyzed or lame were healed" (Acts 8:7). Far from these conversions being a private religious experience, the breaking in of the kingdom in Samaria was manifest and widespread. We read the postscript: "So there was much joy in that city" (Acts 8:8).

The apostle Paul had an urban strategy for mission. He went to the leading cities of a region, boldly announcing the gospel. This included Antioch, Corinth, Ephesus, Philippi, Athens, and Rome.

Consider Paul's mission to Philippi. When Paul cast out the "spirit of a python" indwelling a slave girl, it brought religious and civil unrest to the entire city. This slave girl was a fortune-teller who brought a great deal of profit to her captors, and the exorcism provoked a violent civic reaction: "These men are Jews, and they are disturbing our city" (Acts 16:20). Paul and Barnabas proclaimed the gospel of Christ's kingdom in the marketplace and the merchant class attacked them. For this, the governing authorities then beat and imprisoned them.

Upon release, the apostles moved on to Thessalonica. Once again, their preaching caused social, religious, and political uproar: "These men who have turned the world upside down have come here also" (Acts 17:6). The locals formed a mob and set the city in an uproar.

After Thessalonica, Paul and Barnabas moved onward to Athens. Here Paul secured an audience at the supreme place of public discourse, the Areopagus. Paul preached to the philosophers of the time. He understood this place and these thinkers were at the heart of Greek culture, yet he did not use a philosophical argument—he took on the idols of the land. The invariable aim of kingdom advance is to expose and overthrow the idols of the city. As Paul told them, "Being then God's offspring, we ought not to think that the divine being is like gold or silver or stone, an image formed by the art and imagination of man. The times of ignorance God overlooked . . ." (Acts 17:29–30). Leave idols in place, and nothing changes. Overthrow the idols, and you transform the culture.

Next, Paul moved to Ephesus. With Old Testament force and rapidity, the city was shaken to its foundations. Paul healed and preached, and God acted in might and miracles. This precipitated a massive response of public repentance:

> God was doing extraordinary miracles by the hands of Paul . . . and fear fell upon them all, and the name of the Lord Jesus was extolled. Also many of those who were now believers came, confessing and divulging their practices. And a number of those who had practiced magic arts brought their books together and burned them in the sight of all. And they counted the value of them and found it came to fifty thousand pieces of silver. So the word of the Lord continued to increase and prevail mightily.
>
> ACTS 19:11, 17–20

In the fused socio-political, religious, and economic world of that day, however, nearly all people—merchants, government officials, and religious rulers—were incensed. This public book burning indicated that these citizens were overthrowing their allegiance to the existing order. Religious, political, and economic forces united, infuriated by the intrusion of the message of Christ as Lord:

Demetrius, a silversmith, who made silver shrines of Artemis, brought no little business to the craftsmen. These he gathered together, with the workmen in similar trades, and said, "Men, you know that from this business we have our wealth. And you see and hear that not only in Ephesus but in almost all of Asia this Paul has persuaded and turned away a great many people, saying that gods made with hands are not gods." . . .

When they heard this they were enraged and were crying out, "Great is Artemis of the Ephesians!" So the city was filled with the confusion. . . . Now some cried out one thing, some another, for the assembly was in confusion, and most of them did not know why they had come together.

ACTS 19:24–26, 28–29, 32

In order to reach the world with the gospel, the apostolic strategy was to take the gospel to the heart of the leading cities of the empire where sowing the Good News would have the greatest impact (see Acts 16:12). In a short time, kingdom prayer and bold preaching would shake the foundations undergirding the city.

Historians have recorded the inexorable advance of Christ's kingdom in the centuries following the early-church era. Prayer and evangelism sowed the seeds of societal change. Scholars refer to the many noteworthy exploits of these self-giving Christian believers: nursing victims of plague, reclaiming unwanted infants from garbage heaps, educating the illiterate poor to teach them the doctrines of the faith, building medical facilities, and sending missionaries to establish mission outposts throughout the world. Pagan leaders then sent their children to be educated by the missionary monks, and thousands were converted. The truth marched on.

Yet it would take more than the barbarian hordes to overthrow Rome. When Daniel interpreted Nebuchadnezzar's dream, he described a giant statue representing four successive kingdoms. The head and feet were the great city-kingdoms of Babylon and Rome. It would be that little stone, cut from a mountain, representing the coming of Christ, that would utterly shatter the statue with its iron and clay feet.

> In the days of those kings the God of heaven will set up a kingdom that shall never be destroyed, nor shall the kingdom be left to another people. It shall break in pieces all these kingdoms and bring them to an end, and it shall stand forever, just as you saw that a stone was cut from a mountain by no human hand, and that it broke in pieces the iron, the bronze, the clay, the silver, and the gold.
> DANIEL 2:44–45

Not only Daniel, but all the prophets, including Jesus (see Luke 19:41–44) treated the city—whether Jerusalem, Samaria, Babylon, or Rome—as a kind of person, a living and single collective of its citizens and leaders, with each city having a particular character, way of life, and attitude toward God. With this in mind, we can look at the cities we live in today and assume that Daniel's prophesy (that the city-kingdom of Babylon, and the later city-kingdom of Rome would eventually fall to pieces, conquered by the advance of Christ's kingdom) is still being fulfilled today.

When we talk about a prayer revolution, we mean not only that the Lord of the harvest will grow and revive His church. We mean that wherever Christ's kingdom is proclaimed and received, the surrounding world will be rebuilt.

In North America, for example, the current secular city, with its collective propaganda and technological prowess, imagines itself to be indomitable. Think of the world-shaping influence of Los Angeles when it comes to movies, video games, social and entertainment media—an all-pervasive collective and conglomerate that diverts people from a quest for purpose or meaning. Or consider the economic dominance symbolized in the financial district of lower Manhattan, whose market powers consign an ever-greater portion of the world into a consumer lifestyle.

Though millions bow before the idols of entertainment of a Los Angeles and the envy and acquisition of a New York, these cities' proud sense of unassailable power is an illusion. However strong or pervasive their dominance, or how enduring their hegemony appears, these secular cities still have feet of clay. Like those ancient city-kingdoms of Babylon and Rome, they will one day crumble and fall. If and when God pours out a Spirit of prayer and repentance, the Holy Spirit will send His harvest workers to boldly proclaim the gospel, which will shake the foundations. The steady and relentless advance of Christ through His church will eventually bring the proud city to the ground. Jesus will then send His church to rebuild a new and better city from the rubble (see Isa. 58:12).

That means that we have a job to do. We have a prayer revolution to be part of.

Kingdom-Come Prayer Today

1. Do you believe that prayer and bold public preaching can really challenge the city-kingdoms of today? As you seek urban renewal, ask God to pour out a spirit of prayer on your church and the churches of your city. Pray for "a great number" to turn to the Lord. Ask Christ to give a swelling river of new converts that will become a tide overturning the existing order and nourishing a new world. Ask God how you can sow kingdom seed by marrying acts of justice and kindness with bold and faithful prayer and evangelism.

2. In what ways is your Christian life sowing seeds of the kingdom—working like salt and leaven to penetrate your world? Think it over, you may be surprised.

3. Where do you see evidence of the church proclaiming Christ and doing justice in your city?

The English Awakening (1739 and Following)

On New Year's evening 1739, sixty or seventy Methodists met for Communion and prayer, which was birthed from student gatherings at Oxford. As they prayed long into the night, God's power fell on them and, as John Wesley recalled, they "cried out for exceeding joy, and many fell to the ground," overcome by the power of God, and "broke out with one voice, 'We praise Thee, O God; we acknowledge thee to be Lord.'"[3]

A week later, twenty-two-year-old George Whitefield was ordained, and shortly thereafter he gave his first public sermon in Kingwood, England (a rather barbaric mining town) to two hundred people. The next day, five thousand turned out. A day later, twenty thousand came to hear him.

Out of this revival came the seeds of social renewal, as believers went to the neglected and destitute places of the realm. They preached in the gin alleys, prisons, and madhouses. Where they preached, they sowed seeds of mercy, justice, and good works. Wesley took a humorous view of things: "We are forbidden to go to Newgate [a prison] for fear of making them wicked, and to Bedlam [an insane asylum] for fear of making them mad."[4] Wherever they preached, the Methodists left blankets as well as Bibles. When a jailer was converted, he immediately addressed the desperate conditions in the jail. Christian captors began to show kindness to the captives. Social and political changes of all kinds began to take shape.[5]

These seeds of renewal reaped a harvest and a

remarkable transformation years later in a prison at Bristol. It was now clean and neat, with "no fighting or brawling." There was an unprecedented system of equitable arbitration for prisoners; drunkenness, prostitution, and abuse had been eliminated. Women prisoners were separated from the men. Tools and materials were provided to allow for productive employment, and prisoners received payment from profits on goods sold. The prison held regular church services, prisoners received Bibles as well as free medical services.[6]

Decades later, the seeds of that revival continued to grow and Christian-led transformation of the Western world was transformed when God raised up a man named William Wilberforce who championed the cause of ending child labor and slavery.

PART 3

KINGDOM PRAYER
BREAKS THROUGH

8

HOW A NATION IS RENEWED THROUGH REPENTANCE

Rebuilding church and city starts here

Hope for national revival is a sign that the church is readying for a manifest work of God. When God intends to do a great thing, He gets His people praying. While many forecast a gloomy tomorrow, we turn to the Bible and find that revival is often only a prayer away.

Throughout the pages of the Old Testament, we discover five spectacular national revivals under the kingdoms of Solomon, Asa, Jehoshaphat, Hezekiah, and Josiah. In each case, national awakening initiated and catalyzed when leaders bowed in abject repentance, crying out to God in sorrow and shame. As leaders and people acknowledged and turned from their sins, God answered. The result was a swelling tide of joy and righteousness that filled the land.

In each revival, repentance preceded renewal, just as emptying precedes filling. Those who longed for national revival gathered together and prayed. No detours or shortcuts exist for the healing of our nations; national healing begins with united, humble prayer.

From that day until ours, whenever a national awakening takes place, the revival begins with heart-rending repentance of God's people. God calls His people to confess their own sins, even before they pray on behalf of the nation. He told the Israelites—and tells us too, "If my people who are called by my name humble themselves, and pray and seek my face and turn from their wicked ways, then I will hear from heaven and will forgive their sin and heal their land" (2 Chron. 7:14).

Only after pouring out sincere and deep prayers of repentance for our own sins can Christians move forward and intercede for their nation. To intercede means to pray on behalf of. We cannot expect a lost world to pray for itself; God's people must take the initiative. We must be the "chief repenters" on behalf of the land. It is not enough to point out and decry the evils of the day; we need to intercede—to repent on behalf of our fellow citizens and to recognize our own complicity in the national sin. When we pray for our nation and its cities, we identify with our fellow citizens and confess our "wicked ways." Judgment begins with the people of God. So does revival.

I have attended prayer breakfasts crowded with politicians and dignitaries. Often prayer starts and finishes by thanking God that we are in a free country and then we ask Him to bless us with continued prosperity. In other words, we ask God not to disrupt the existing order, but to bless and prosper the status quo. There is little awe of God and a distinct absence of repentance. We seldom are penitent for our offenses against God or humankind, or cry out for those who feel the sting of poverty, the lash of injustice, or the pain of oppression. This is not kingdom prayer.

In fact the Bible has a great deal to say about how we should pray for our land and repent of its sins. It tells us that we are to pray faithfully for God to bless those who rule and govern in church, state, courts, and centers of education, that they will establish and enforce just laws, that they will labor for peace, in order that we may live godly lives and that the gospel will advance and prosper in our land (see 1 Tim. 2:1–4).

Discerning Christians do not pray for a mere continuance of the current secular state of our nation. Crying out for the advance of the gospel and the free proclamation of the truth are embedded within the scope of kingdom prayer for our land. As we shall see in the following biblical examples, when God's people cry out for heartfelt repentance, it marks the headwaters for rivers of national revival.

If we follow the guideline of 2 Chronicles 7:14, we have no danger of finger pointing and self-righteous accusation when we pray for leaders and against evil in our land. God's Word to Solomon provides the perfect solution: as we intercede for our nation, we confess "our" sins and wickedness and identify with those we pray for.[1]

OLD TESTAMENT KINGDOM ERA REVIVALS

The time from King Saul to the Babylonian captivity is the biblical era of Kings. Second Chronicles begins with King Solomon's reign and narrates centuries of national awakenings. With each revival, when righteous kings called upon the Lord and the people cried out to God in repentance, God answered their prayers and sent the promised healing. Idols were dismantled, fear of the Lord reinstated, and healing and joy filled the land. But not all of Israel's kings were righteous.

In the chart below we see a distinction between "good" and

"bad" kings. The decisive factor in this delineation is the fact that those kings who led the nation to repentance were good and the unrepentant were bad. Some of the kings, like Solomon, started well but finished poorly.

Let's look at these five kingdom-era revivals so we can learn and emulate what repentant prayer revolution looks like, and then by following the kings' guidance, we can bring renewal and revival to our own land.

1. Revival in Solomon's Day Began with a Great Prayer

Revival history begins with King Solomon's majestic prayer for the nation at the temple dedication. After Solomon was established in royal splendor, having inherited a period of peace from his father, King David, Solomon designed, erected, decorated, and dedicated a stunning temple as the first permanent worship center to God. The prayer of dedication he offered at its grand opening became a prayer for the ages. King Solomon prayed not only for the people of his day but also for Israel throughout its history.

In this panoramic prayer, Solomon prophesied the inevitable judgments resulting from the neglect of God and His law—drought, famine, plague, warfare, defeat, and captivity. He pleaded

EVALUATING KINGS OF JUDAH		
GOOD	BAD	MIX OF GOOD & BAD
Solomon		
Rehoboam		
Abijam		
Asa		
Jehoshaphat		
Jehoram		
Ahaziah		
Athaliah queen		
Joash		
Amaziah		
Azariah (Uzziah)		
Jotham		
Ahaz		
Hezekiah		
Manasseh		
Amon		
Josiah		
Johoahaz (Shallum)		
Jehoiakim		
Jehoiachin		
Zedekiah		

with God, asking that, no matter how far His people strayed, God would hear their humble and repentant prayer and restore them to life and joy.

Here is a summary of Solomon's prayer for the nation:

> If there is famine in the land, if there is pestilence or blight or mildew or locust or caterpillar, if their enemies besiege them in the land at their gates, whatever plague, whatever sickness there is, whatever prayer, whatever plea is made by any man or by all your people Israel, each knowing his own affliction and his own sorrow and stretching out his hands toward this house, then hear from heaven your dwelling place and forgive.... Likewise, when a foreigner, who is not of your people Israel, comes ... and prays toward this house, hear from heaven your dwelling place ... in order that all the peoples of the earth may know your name and fear you....
>
> If they sin against you—for there is no one who does not sin ... so that they are carried away captive to a land far or near ... if they repent with all their heart and with all their soul ... and pray ... then hear from heaven your dwelling place their prayer and their pleas, and maintain their cause and forgive your people who have sinned against you.
>
> 2 CHRONICLES 6:28–30, 32–33, 36, 38–39

This prayer was filled with longing for God as well as longing for revival. As soon as Solomon finished—and amid a chorus of trumpet-heralding priests and jubilant singers—God answered with the burning glory of His presence. Fire came down from heaven and consumed the burnt offering and the sacrifices. Then God's splendor and presence filled the temple to overflowing:

"The priests could not enter the house of the LORD, because the glory of the LORD filled the LORD's house" (2 Chron. 7:2). What a remarkable scene of God's pleasure and presence, a foreshadowing of the future great day when the temple would be shaken again, after the final sacrifice was offered at nearby Calvary!

Pleased with Solomon's prayer for Israel, God spoke a promise for the ages, guaranteeing national healing and renewal from the very day that His people turn from their sin in repentant prayer: "You will seek me and find me, when you seek me with all your heart" (Jer. 29:13).

God promises forgiveness and healing; however, there must first be repentance. Repentance is a matter of the heart. In biological terms, when the arteries of a human heart become clogged with foreign and pathological elements, the only option is surgery to restore the proper flow of blood throughout the body. In the same way, the arteries of a nation become blocked by unrepentant sin. Idolatry in its various forms—sexual immorality, neglect of the poor, corruption, bribery, murder, greed, and envy—clog the arteries of a country's health and strangle life of its joy and meaning. Eventually, death is imminent, and the only hope for healing is radical, open-heart surgery.

> **The renewal of a nation begins and advances with the inner transformation of one person at a time.**

When we repent, we cry out for an entirely supernatural work within—that God would remove our dying works and words and replace them with the holy resolves of His Spirit. Revival begins when we ask God to fill us with His Holy Spirit and He answers yes! As He tells us through His prophet:

> I will give you a new heart, and a new spirit I will put
> within you. And I will remove the heart of stone from your
> flesh and give you a heart of flesh . . . and cause you to walk
> in my statutes and be careful to obey my rules.
>
> EZEKIEL 36:26–27

Revival begins within and then moves outward. The renewal of a nation begins and advances with the inner transformation of one person at a time.

As we shall see, Solomon's pattern of intercessory prayer and God's gracious response repeated throughout Israel's history. King after king and prayer after prayer echoed the spirit of Solomon's petition.

Sadly, Solomon's revival was brief. In his old age, Solomon led the nation into worshiping other gods. His son Rehoboam hastened the fall: "When the rule of Rehoboam was established and he was strong, he abandoned the law of the LORD, and all Israel with him" (2 Chron. 12:1). Rehoboam's arrogance and rebellion precipitated the divided kingdom, as he cast off all God's commands in more egregious ways than had been done before (see 1 Kings 14:22). He left a legacy of idolatry, oppression, and cult prostitution. His son Abijam continued in his father's footsteps.

2. Revival under King Asa

After twenty years of decline under Rehoboam and Abijam, repentant prayer arose again, this time from King Asa. A crisis precipitated the awakening. Confronted by an innumerable army, King Asa called upon the Lord, as the odds appeared hopeless:

> O LORD, there is none like you to help, between the
> mighty and the weak. Help us, O LORD our God, for we
> rely on you, and in your name we have come against this

multitude. O LORD, you are our God; let not man prevail against you.

2 CHRONICLES 14:11

In astounding fashion, God answered Asa's prayer. A huge army was routed without drawing a sword or throwing a spear. The only work left for Israel's troops was to gather the spoils. Strengthened by the words of a prophet, Asa stirred the people to bear fruits of repentance. He removed the idols, restored temple worship, and renewed the covenant. Justice and mercy met, and joy was restored as the people "swore an oath to the LORD . . . with all their heart and had sought him with their whole desire, and he was found by them" (2 Chron. 15:14–15).

The Jewish people enjoyed rest from their enemies as the fires of grace warmed the land for the next thirty-five years.

When God calls His people to engage with the world, He musters His troops for war (see Rev. 19:11–16). Throughout the ages the songs we sing capture the military nature of our mission, stirring us to follow Christ into the fray. Songs such as "A Mighty Fortress Is Our God," "The Battle Belongs to the Lord," "God of the City," and "Onward, Christian Soldiers" rouse our hearts and move our feet to engage the enemy. Consider the words of this hymn:

> Lead on, O King eternal,
> till sin's fierce war shall cease,
> and holiness shall whisper
> the sweet amen of peace.
> For not with swords' loud clashing
> or roll of stirring drums;
> with deeds of love and mercy
> the heavenly kingdom comes.[2]

While our warfare is not with gunfire or horsepower, it is still military in nature. The enemies we face each day are the opponents of the gospel and the unseen forces that lead people away from God. Our weapons are power-filled words of witness and Spirit-forged works of kindness and mercy. Chief in a believer's arsenal is prayer.

3. Revival under King Jehoshaphat

Asa's son Jehoshaphat improved upon his father's prayer and resolve: he "sought the God of his father and walked in his commandments. . . . His heart was courageous in the ways of the LORD. And furthermore, he took the high places and the Asherim out of Judah" (2 Chron. 17:4, 6).

When "a great multitude" waged war against Judah, like his father, Jehoshaphat turned to God in prayer. On this day, not only the king, but everyone in the land, including the priests, temple servants, and singers, along with all the people of Judah, called out to God in mighty prayer and praise:

> "[We] built for you . . . a sanctuary for your name, saying, 'If disaster comes upon us, the sword, judgment, or pestilence, or famine, we will stand before this house and before you—for your name is in this house—and cry out to you in our affliction, and you will hear and save.' . . . Meanwhile all Judah stood before the LORD, with their little ones, their wives, and their children. . . . Then Jehoshaphat bowed his head with his face to the ground, and all Judah and the inhabitants of Jerusalem fell down before the LORD, worshiping the LORD. And the Levites . . . stood up to praise the LORD, the God of Israel, with a very loud voice. . . . And when they began to sing and praise, the LORD set an ambush.
>
> 2 CHRONICLES 20:8–9, 13, 18–19, 22

The vast host arrayed against God's people was defeated without a casualty. A lasting peace set in. Once again the city knew renewal and the temple experienced revival: "So the realm of Jehoshaphat was quiet, for his God gave him rest all around" (2 Chron. 20:30).

Following Jehoshaphat's reign, under King Jehoram, King Ahaziah, and Queen Athaliah, a spiritual winter set in. These royals halted the revival and plummeted Judah to new depths of idolatry and degradation, such that for the next 130 years only a few brief periods of renewal occurred.

This era of death came to its terminus with King Ahaz, who famously cast off all restraint. In an all-out show of contempt for the Holy One of Israel, he outdid even the original nations of Canaan in immoral acts and social evil. Ahaz worshiped Baal, practiced child sacrifice, and even sacrificed his own sons "according to the abominations of the nations whom the LORD drove out before the people of Israel" (2 Chron. 28:3). God gave up Ahaz and Judah to their enemies; tens of thousands were slaughtered in battles with Syria and Samaria, and even more were taken captive.

Still, a beautiful redemptive story took place within this depressing account of national and spiritual mayhem. After winning a battle, the soldiers of the northern kingdom of Israel captured a great crowd of the people of Judah. They led their fellow Jews, chained and naked, into captivity. They intended to make slaves of them, but God intervened and sent a prophet who warned them against their intent to imprison their fellow citizens. Israel heeded God and repented; instead of imprisonment, they provided their brothers and sisters with food and clothing, anointed them with healing oil, and sent them home with gifts and provisions (see 2 Chron. 28:4ff). This breakthrough of love and kindness helped Israel look forward to her future liberation from the slavery of sin and the restoration of a new and unified humanity in Christ (see Eph. 2:13–22).

The stage was now set for the greatest king and the greatest awakening since Solomon. Hezekiah, son of Ahaz, would offer a prayer that led the nation into a great revival.

4. Awakening under King Hezekiah

From the day he became king, Hezekiah set his heart to follow God. He cleansed the temple of its idols, restored temple worship, and renewed the covenant by celebrating the Passover. Joy sprang up from the city streets and prayers ascended to heaven: "So there was great joy in Jerusalem, for since the time of Solomon the son of David king of Israel there had been nothing like this in Jerusalem. . . . And their voice was heard, and their prayer came to his holy habitation in heaven" (2 Chron. 30:26–27).

Some years later, a watershed event precipitated a mighty renewal. Hezekiah and the city of Jerusalem were surrounded by the greatest army in the world. Assyria had set its sights on Jerusalem (see Isa. 36–39). King Sennacherib besieged Jerusalem and mocked God: "He wrote letters to cast contempt on the LORD . . . saying, 'Like the gods of the nations of the lands who have not delivered their people from my hands, so the God of Hezekiah will not deliver his people from my hand'" (2 Chron. 32:17).

Hezekiah did not respond directly to Sennacherib; rather, he responded by praying to God "because of this and cried to heaven" (2 Chron. 32:20), and God answered in majesty and power. As with previous revivals, they won the battle without a single weapon! The Assyrians scattered, and Sennacherib's own sons killed him. The land received peace and healing, and for the next thirty years, justice and righteousness flowed like a river.

Today, with the church surrounded by detractors and mockers, we are reminded not to focus our attention on our enemies but to fix our gaze on almighty God. Prayers of faith are not a reaction to persecution; rather, they are birthed from a deep trust in God's actions that He will always defend His name and His church.

Following Hezekiah, Mannasah and Amon led the nation into a six-decade night of godless and lawless ways. Only a few dutiful priests remained. The temple lay neglected. The book of God's law gathered dust. The nation fell back into idolatry, child sacrifice, temple prostitution, occult practices, neglect of the needy, and oppression of the poor (see 2 Chron. 33:1–6). Repentance was missing, and every form of sin clogged the nation's heart until the land died.

5. Revival under King Josiah

In spite of Judah's wickedness, God was not finished with His people, for His loving kindness endures forever. God raised a young man to intercede on behalf of the nation. When only sixteen, Josiah began to seek the Lord (see 2 Chron. 34:3). Pleased with Josiah's prayer, God answered immediately. A message of hope came through Huldah, the prophetess:

> "Because your heart was tender and you humbled yourself before God when you heard his words against this place and its inhabitants, and you have humbled yourself before me and have torn your clothes and wept before me, I also have heard you," declares the LORD.
>
> 2 CHRONICLES 34:27

Cheered by this word, Josiah brought the nation into a covenant renewal ceremony. The people gladly joined the revival. A joyous Passover reflected the national heart of repentance: "No Passover like it had been kept in Israel since the days of Samuel the prophet" (2 Chron. 35:18). As with previous revivals, God's challenge and promise to Solomon (see 2 Chron. 7:14) came to pass. Josiah and the people confessed and turned from their sin, and God healed the land. Praise filled the temple and the city as they worshiped God and restored justice. The nation resounded with rejoicing.

IF THE CHURCH IS IN TROUBLE, SO IS THE NATION

We can have no national revival in our day until God's people learn to weep for their sin and shame, and cry out for their nation. Wherever and whenever the people heed God's call to repent of their own sin, the promise of national revival has already begun.

What about the state of Christianity in our nations today? Are things that bad? We might look back at the godless, lawless people of Kings and Chronicles and be rightfully horrified, yet a closer examination reveals parallels that are impossible to ignore. For example, not unlike the six-decade decline before Josiah, we can look back at the church in Canada over the past sixty years and see a steady decline into darkness. If we have the honesty and courage to face it, it is a bleak picture.

In our day, no less than in Josiah's day, the knowledge of God and His Word have been gathering dust and religion has steadily declined. For example, more than half of Canadians attended church in 1960. In 1986, 43 percent of Canadians said they attended religious services at least once a month. In 2015, that number has dropped to 23 percent.[3] According to Gallup polls, the church in the United States is also in decline. In 1950, 62 percent of Americans went to church. By 2013 the number had declined to 52 percent.[4] While in 1990, some 70 percent of Americans were members of a church, in 2019 this number dropped to 50 percent.[5]

At the same time, in both countries, prayer meetings have declined in frequency and numbers. There is a "graying" of the prayer meetings that remain. And in the home, Scripture reading and prayer have become relics of a once-robust Christian faith. When we do pray, our prayers are often weak in worship and turned in on ourselves. Too often our prayers exhibit little intercession and no repentance for our sins and for our nation. Listen to our prayers and it can seem as if it is God's responsibility to serve us rather than us serving Him. It is becoming rare to find prayer meetings for world mission and for the persecuted church. Sunday morning churchgoing has gradually replaced a vital Christianity. In a word, we look a lot like Israel in decline.

If we overlay the world of Judah's decline over our world today, we find many parallels. In that day, they worshiped idols. While we do not have statues to misrepresent God, we passionately worship our own inventions. Our idols and attachments are not overtly religious in nature, but they are religious in observance. Our devotion to entertainment and our reverence for technology is the new idolatry. We create an infinite variety of ways to devote our every spare moment to "the lust of the flesh, the lust of the eyes, and the pride of life" (1 John 2:16 NKJV).

We may not overtly worship false gods, but we ignore God altogether. Step by step, decree by decree, the knowledge of God is being edited from the public square, school, and our collective mind. Portrayed as neutral, our secular devotion has become a cover-up for mere atheism. To be an atheist, by definition, is to be godless. Atheism in our day often expresses itself as contempt for anyone foolish enough to believe in God or affirm His righteous laws.

The wicked kings of Judah practiced child sacrifice, killing their own children to satisfy the devouring gods they worshiped. For decades, we have allowed unrestricted abortion of unborn children.

In Canada, in 2018, applicants for certain government grants had to sign a document supporting abortion or be denied funding.[6]

Beginning in June 2017, Canada now permits killing the aged and infirm. In British Columbia, hospital policies prohibit their employees from advising assisted-suicide applicants against taking their own life. Within the first seventeen months of legalizing physician-assisted suicide, more than two thousand Canadians were killed by medical procedure! In the six months following, there was a 30 percent increase with 1,523 reported suicides.[7]

The Israelites were guilty of sexual sin. They implemented temple prostitution—male and female, homosexual and heterosexual—practiced religious orgies, and committed adultery on a massive scale. In Canada and the United States, we say sexual practices are a "private matter" and seek to keep the government out of the bedroom. In the process, we close our eyes to adultery and promiscuity. Women, girls, men, and boys are exploited and trafficked into pornography and prostitution. Countless numbers, from the youngest age, are addicted to pornography. We dismiss God's created order for gender distinction as we embrace, promote, and legislate personal gender selection.

When evil kings reigned over Judah, false prophets praised the existing order and maintained the corrupt system. Today, we have our own false prophets, inescapable in the vast networks of news sources, entertainment outlets, and advertising media that provide propaganda to flatter our desire for autonomy and self-indulgence.

One way to describe sin is to say that *each one has gone his or her own way.* Freedom in our time and place often means only self-determination. We despise any infringement on our autonomy. In consequence, we become godless and lawless—this is the root "wickedness" referred to in 2 Chronicles 7:14. This is our legacy of sin and justification for God's wrath. And this is why we need national repentance.

It is not only the secular world around us, today's Christians have rebelled against God's law. God's call to repentance and the promise of healing speaks as loudly today as it did in Old Testament times: "If my people who are called by my name humble themselves, and pray and seek my face and turn from their wicked ways, then I will hear from heaven and will forgive their sin and heal their land" (2 Chron. 7:14).

WHAT DOES PRAYER FOR NATIONAL REVIVAL LOOK LIKE TODAY?

In the summer of 2017, Prayer Current held two-day prayer workshops in three different cities in India with Serve India, the Council of Reformed Churches in India, and the West Delhi Pastors Association. At the heart of our time together, we broke into groups of seven and looked at the Lord's Prayer. Each person was assigned one of the seven parts of this prayer and instructed to discern the kingdom purpose behind the petition. The interaction was energetic, as these leaders realized that the Lord's Prayer is Jesus' guide and framework for all of His kingdom purposes. For example, "Your will be done" implies not only that we pray to love and submit to the will of the Father, but also that we seek to carry out His will by doing justice and mercy. In India, this meant praying about how to serve widows and orphans, praying against the caste system, and resolving to treat everyone with dignity. This is how we prayed.

For each part of the prayer, a different person shared his or her insights and then the whole group prayed through the prayer. The volume increased with fervent intensity as the group prayed.

In Visakhapatnam, when we neared the end of our time to-gether, we circled the large room to pray for the church of India and for the nation. First we faced one another, lifted our hands, and with one voice and one heart, prayed for one another and the church. As the Spirit deepened, the prayer increased in loud and joyous unity. Children playing outside came in to see what was happening, and they too lifted their hands to join in.

After the prayer subsided, we fellowshiped over chai tea. After tea, once again we circled the room. This time, hands raised, we faced outward and began to pray for India. I coached, "Wherever you are facing, pray for that region and its cities." With one voice, the assembly raised a cry to God for the land of India: prayers for salvation, for mercy, for justice and deliverance for the oppressed, for God to restrain wicked oppressors. Longing and hope were written on their faces as these people prayed for God to heal their land, forgive their sins, bring salvation to many, compel leaders to fear God, and protect the poor from oppression. One of the bish-ops raised a beautiful, sonorous voice in a well-known song for the church and the nation. The worship team joined in. Hands raised and hearts lifted, we sang and prayed with a single voice. Some knelt and others swayed with the music, united in full-throated song and full spectrum of emotions. I believe we were all thinking the same thing, *This is kingdom prayer. This is what you made us for, Lord.*

We can follow this practice in any meeting. "Circling up" and directing our prayers inward for the church and outward for the nation brings embodiment to our love for one another and for all those who do not know Christ. Believers everywhere rejoice in the opportunity to humbly and urgently pray for the church and the nation that renewal through repentance may come.

Kingdom-Come Prayer Today

1. If revival starts with earnest, united, repentant prayer, ask yourself and discuss with others the following questions:

   • In three of the Old Testament revivals studied, the enemy army is defeated by God, without human agency. What are the lessons in this for our times?

   • How bad are things today? Does this assessment of present evil and call to repentance ring true or is it overblown? How can we tell?

   • How much of our prayers are cries of repentance? In what ways can we begin to incorporate this into our prayers?

   • In what ways can we gather together to pray for our nation and confess our personal and national sins to God?

2. For a practical and simple exercise on praying for the heart of your nation, see Appendix C.

The Welsh Revival (1904)

For three months, deep into the middle of each night, Evan Roberts, a college student in Wales, prayed for revival. While praying, he heard God's promise that many thousands would be saved. Then one Sunday evening in 1904, Evan preached his first sermon in his home village of Lougher in which he called his seventeen hearers to repentance and consecration. The Spirit moved, revival began and quickly spread.

Soon entire congregations fell on their knees in fervent prayer. The awakening changed not only believers, but entire communities. The London *Times* stated:

> The whole population had been suddenly stirred by a common impulse. Religion had become the absorbing interest of their lives. They had gathered at crowded services for six and eight hours at a time. Political meetings and even football matches were postponed . . . quarrels between trade-union workmen and non-unionists had been made up. . . . At Glyn-Neath a feud had existed for the past 10 or 12 years between the two Independent chapels, but during the past week united services have been held in both chapels, and the ministers have shaken hands before the congregations.[8]

Judges were presented with white gloves signifying no cases to be tried. Alcoholism was halved. Those normally untouched by the ministry of the church came to Christ. Employers noticed a great improvement in their employees' work. In fact, one mine manager said, "The haulers are some of the very lowest. They have driven their horses by obscenity and kicks.

Now they can hardly persuade their horses to start working, because they have no obscenity and kicks."[9]

Witness to the revival, David Matthews described the power of what was happening:

> Everything sprang into new life. Former blasphemers were the most eloquent, both in prayer and praise. . . . Drunkards forgot the way to saloons . . . they were busy worshiping. . . . It was the young people who responded with the greatest alacrity to the challenge of absolute surrender and consecrated to the service of the Lord.[10]

The Welsh Revival brought in more than 100,000 converts and was the farthest-reaching movement of the general awakening, for it affected the whole of the evangelical cause in India, Korea, and China, renewed revival in Japan and South Africa, and sent a wave of awakening over Africa, Latin America, and the South Seas. Yet as author James Edwin Orr explained:

> The early twentieth century Evangelical Awakening . . . did not begin with the phenomenal Welsh Revival of 1904–05. Rather its sources were in the springs of little prayer meetings which seemed to arise spontaneously all over the world, combining into streams of expectation which became a river of blessing in which the Welsh Revival became the greatest cataract.[11]

Each prayer gathering was a little revival. As these prayer gatherings multiplied and converged, revival momentum increased until a fast flowing tide of ascension power covered the land.

9

HOW IDOLS ARE REMOVED THROUGH KINGDOM PRAYER

Kingdom prayer discerns and expels prevailing idolatry

In the Old Testament, as we surveyed in the previous chapter, when it comes to idols, it is a matter of "search and destroy." Righteous kings and devout people not only avoided the idols of the land, they did not rest until they were removed and demolished. The death grip of idols broke through humble, repentant prayer—and nothing else! Idols were rendered obsolete and worthy only of contempt: "Then you will defile your carved idols overlaid with silver and your gold-plated metal images. You will scatter them as unclean things. You will say to them, 'Be gone!'" (Isa. 30:22). Once this death grip was broken, the people returned to the life-giving joy of prayer, worship, fellowship, and justice.

The church still battles with idols. We still "search and destroy" but in a different manner. In one sense the whole Christian life is a battle with idols, for it is a battle for our hearts, minds, and imaginations. At its most basic level, an idol is any object, image, person, or idea that usurps God as the primary object of our devotion. Even if a person claims to be agnostic or atheist, they devote and attach themselves to images and ideals they hope will satisfy their needs and aspirations. If someone disavows faith in God or gods, they cannot help but attach their innate capacity for worship onto something or someone. Whatever becomes the supreme object of their heart's devotion is their god.

The inner war against idols is fought with prayer. Each of us fights the battle one skirmish at a time, with one prayer at a time. Prayer opens the inner sanctuary of our hearts to the Father's influence and filling. In the process what is empty and worthless is expelled. For this reason, the simple act of genuine prayer is a revolutionary assault on the ensnaring powers of idols.

For example, if you have an idolatrous attachment to digital technology, whenever you withdraw and set aside meaningful time for conversation with God, you are, at the same time, disconnecting from the temptations and urgent pleadings of the world around you. In order to spend time in conversation with God, you "hang up" on the world—you set aside your cellphone, ignore social media in all its forms, and otherwise stop being entertained. The very act of genuine prayer breaks the hold. As you walk with God, and experience the revelations and fillings of His Spirit, you will no longer lust for the barren facsimile the world offers.

The critical factor in your ability to expel idols is that you be filled with a surpassing powerful and joyous experience of God— the hunger and thirst of every regenerated heart. God promises your hunger and thirst will be satisfied, and you will be delivered from your idols as you cry out to Him in prayer. As God said through the psalmist, "Call upon me in the day of trouble; I will deliver you, and you shall glorify me" (Ps. 50:15).

IDOLS OLD AND NEW

In most ancient cities the city center was reserved for the temples and objects of worship, while the surrounding countryside housed shrines devoted to lesser gods. With deep devotion, worshipers entered these shrines to their idols and offered sacrifices, burned incense, spoke prayers, paid dues, and practiced rites and rituals. In ancient times, temple prostitution and orgies were often part of the ceremony, especially when the god or goddess represented forces of fertility.

To seek out the idols of our cultures today, we need only pay a visit to the heart of a major city. It is here we find the objects of worship on full display. For example, you can find a massive temple dedicated to Buddha at the center of Thailand's Chiang Mai. Or consider Malaysia's capital city, Kuala Lumpur.

Several years ago twenty-five Christian leaders and I met for a two-day prayer summit in this city. Together, we went for an afternoon tour. When we arrived downtown, we discovered not a mosque or temple but massive twin towers of finance and retail. Though its people are very religious—61 percent of Malaysians practice Islam, 19 percent are Buddhists, 9 percent Christians, and 6 percent Hindu[1]—there was no temple where we might expect to find it. Instead, the Petronas Twin Towers, for many years the tallest skyscrapers in the world, stand more than eighty stories high and house the financial, technological, and business offices that power a global economy. It takes little imagination to deduce the idolatries fed by these engines of industry.

What captured our attention, however, was not only the skyscrapers. Centered between the two towers, in the innermost chambers of this city, is a massive shopping mall filled with inviting, sexualized images of affluence and beauty.

Location matters, and in most modern cities, like the ancient cities before them, the culture's temple resides in the center. The innermost chambers of the temple house the sanctum sanctorum where the chief idol resides. As we gathered, like thousands of Malaysians, at the air-conditioned, glittering shopping center inside the Petronas Towers, we realized we had stumbled upon a place of worship.

This is the heart of Kuala Lumpur. We intuited something important about the place, so we paused to pray in front of the impressive towers. We had come to admire the stunning architectural wonder, as well as to understand the aspirations of the people of Kuala Lumpur. We assumed that a view from the top of the Petronas Towers would give us a clue, but it turned out that much of our mission would be accomplished by surveying the city from ground level.

We headed down a set of stairs into the mall where we found people of many faiths and nationalities calmly milling about, sharing a collective experience of accessing global retailers—Victoria's Secret, Hugo Boss, TAG Heuer, among others—and anticipating the status inferred upon them as purchasers of global name-brand prestige. Floor to ceiling, glittering images of beautiful men and women, unstained by the hardships of life, exuded eternal youth and beauty. These images' searching gaze, slightly parted lips, and artfully positioned limbs were charged with seductive sexual energy and promiscuous availability. Perfectly proportioned mannequins and exquisitely designed display cases resembled their own brand of graven images.

They were not unlike the carvings of gods, ample-bodied and suggestively postured, found at many Hindu temples. Their eyes invite you into their world, suggesting, *This can be yours! Yes, it costs, but how satisfying to walk among the glorious icons of our culture!* Their bodily presence, in the form of mannequin and marketing, calls out for worship of eternal youth, bodily perfection, physical beauty, earthly affluence, and celebrity fame.

Our experience of this visual extravaganza incited many questions: What does all this glamour—the shiny steel, architectural achievement, and flawless images—signify? What does it say about the heart of Kuala Lumpur (and the hearts of most modern cities with similar places of worship)? How did a mall come to be located at the heart and center of a religious city and who gave permission? While we might assume that something seemingly innocuous as a shopping mall poses no threat to the city's mosques and churches, its strategic location and remarkable structure represent much more than a mere convenient shopping hub.

Materialism produces material images. The images of an electronic culture are powerful and seductive. They shine with beauty and entice us with a legion of unspoken promises. The reality is that the world's shiny screens and alluring images have already captured the hearts of humankind—not only secularists, but also pious Muslims, Hindus, Buddhists, and Christians. A splendid mall, along with its manmade images, is permitted to occupy the center of the city because it has already proven stronger than the power of other gods. Not that the other gods have been eliminated. The cohabitation of secular idols and images alongside the religions of the world demonstrates syncretism and accommodation. The promise is made: *You can keep your gods, just give us your heart.*

Juxtaposing this scene at Petronas Towers with my recent visit to India, I realized that my feelings of discomfort upon entering the mall were not dissimilar to those I had when touring a temple in India. Devout Hindus go to the temple to secure favor and a better life. They may have selfish or even sinister motives in wanting to solicit help from the deity. The same could be said of most nominally religious people: whether through ritual or prayer, they seek celestial favors in the form of status, sex, wealth, or power. This is exactly what a mall-as-temple promises with all its images of eternal youth, sexual beauty, and attainable affluence: *Drink deep of this well. Buy in. All you need are new clothes, better cosmetics, and the latest technology, and then your dreams will come true. Everything you desire can be yours.*

Secular materialism breeds material gods, whether in the form of shiny images or technological prowess. One might argue, "Come on, these are just photos of good-looking people. They have no religious content or meaning. How can you call them idols?" The Bible says otherwise. Images of the ancient gods were just inert wood, metal, and stone. Similarly, idols on mall display or computer screen are lifeless, no matter how colorful and realistic they are. They have no real existence apart from the view of those devoted to them. As Isaiah said, "Behold, you are nothing, and your work is less than nothing" (Isa. 41:24). Idolatry is in the eye of the beholder.

These facts yield a stunning revelation. If an idol is unreal, then nothing promised by serving the idol is real either. Attach yourself to anything but God and you will never be satisfied. When God warns you to stop thirsting for nothing, put away your idols, because He has your good in mind. He wants you to be filled to overflowing with the ever-increasing power and joy of His presence. Jesus used a metaphor from daily life to say the same thing: "Everyone who drinks of this water will be thirsty again, but whoever drinks of the water that I will give him will never be thirsty again. The water that I will give him will become in him a spring of water welling up to eternal life" (John 4:13–14). Long for what the world offers and you will end up parched. Seek the life of God's Spirit and your longings will forever be filled to overflowing.

THE POWER OF MAMMON

It is a mistake to underestimate materialism. In Milton's *Paradise Lost,* the demon Mammon is one of the few gods to rival Satan in might and magnificence. *Mammon* is the old English word for materialism. A glimmering and sanitized mall presents the perfect place for Mammon to hide out. In his allegorical work *The Pilgrim's Progress,* John Bunyan depicted such a place as Vanity Fair:

> *I saw in my dream, that when they were got out of the wilderness, they presently saw a town before them, and the name of that town is Vanity; and at the town there is a fair kept, called Vanity Fair; it is kept all the year long. It beareth the name of Vanity Fair because the town where it is kept is lighter than vanity; and, also because all that is there sold, or that cometh thither, is vanity. As is the saying of the wise, "all that cometh is vanity."[2]*

As Bunyan pointed out, "The way to the Celestial City lies just through this town where this lusty fair is kept."[3] Moreover, Bunyan noted that the pilgrim believers became martyrs when they decried the idolatry of Vanity Fair's commerce, lusts, and indulgences.

A binary, incestuous relationship often exists between commerce and idolatry. Consider the many warnings Jesus gave His disciples about the powerful seduction of wealth and affluence.[4] Consider also Paul's confrontation with the Ephesian merchants and idol craftsmen. When the gospel was preached in Ephesus, former idol worshipers confessed faith in Christ, renounced their idolatry, and destroyed their idolatrous images and books in a massive bonfire (see Acts 19:18–20). Yet this public affirmation of Christ infuriated the guild of craftsmen, not just for religious reasons, but also because of potential financial ruin (see Acts 19:23–27).

In Ephesus, and in any city, bold public proclamation and widespread reception of the Good News can serve to unmask and destroy the hold of idols. In comparison with the value of getting to know Jesus, idols and magic incantations are useless and detestable.

Today, the same truth applies—what the world offers is a cheap "knock-off" of what is real and genuine. Only Jesus can fulfill the deepest needs of our hearts: "That my joy may be in you, and that your joy may be full" (John 15:11).

THE SECULAR AGE AND OUR VIEW OF GOD

While formerly many cultures produced idols that resembled a human likeness, the idols did not represent man, they represented the gods. But in our day and time, there is no god-reference to our idolatry; humanity is forming images of humanity itself. Instead of God expelling idols, our idols expel God. Take, for example, our fascination with pictures of the natural world. Images are displayed with no acknowledgment of God. This world was once believed to be the domain of God—His creation. Now in the public space of our secular age, the very idea of creation is vigorously dismissed. Everything on earth is believed to have evolved on its own. The world that was once owned by God we now claim for ourselves. In a secular culture, we have no need for images or words about God. In fact, to seriously intrude faith in God desecrates the modern enterprise. Just as there is a sense of trespass when a non-Hindu enters a Hindu temple, so too does mention of God as Creator and Sovereign trespass on the inner sanctuary of our modern idol industry.

Men and women today still produce images of what they worship. The fact that most of our representations are of people indicate that humankind's idol today is humanity itself. In biblical language, today has become the age of man, where "the man of lawlessness is revealed . . . who opposes and exalts himself against every so-called god or object of worship" (2 Thess. 2:3–4).

This yields a profound observation: we have become our own gods! In our secular age we have chosen to pour our religious affections, hopes, and longings onto ourselves. We look to ourselves, our leaders in technology, science, and medicine, educators, politicians and policy makers for deliverance in times of trouble and to take us to a new future. We reason that because there is no God in heaven, we must take up His rule and reign and become our own gods.

HOW IMAGES BECOME IDOLS

The second of the Ten Commandments forbids making man-made images. These "graven images" are merely objects and pictures that we make. They become an idol when they demand our attention and when we attach our hearts' affections and hopes to them. As in the Malaysian mall, the proliferation of man-made images cannot but capture our hearts and imaginations. In time, these images take over, and we can become irretrievably attached, even addicted, to what they represent. Images become idols.

I recall a striking picture of the power of images at the Petronas Mall. We had ascended a few floors to upper levels. Looking down, we saw that virtually everyone was gazing intently at his or her cellphone.

Computers and mobile technology provide an infinite variety of man-made "graven images." Take, for example, the smartphone with all its technological wonder—interactive applications, communications, entertainment, games, and social media. Like a hungry chick that demands constant attention, the cellphone calls out to us repeatedly, and we hasten to reply. We eagerly await the next notification. We check our phones constantly to stay connected or to fill downtime. It takes scant argument to prove we have become attached, even addicted, to our smartphones and the images they provide.

Underlying the expression of the smartphone lays our culture's greatest idol, the chief god of our secular pantheon: technology itself. Our ability to manipulate the environment, observe the vast reaches of the heavens, study the subatomic world, alter our genes, provide unlimited comfort, and even stave off death, allows us to foolishly imagine that we are now the sole masters of our world and can reconfigure our own destiny. We have no need of God. We were once content to be tenants of the vineyard owned by another Lord, but the time has come for us to expel the Owner and claim the vineyard for ourselves: "When the tenants saw the son, they said to themselves, 'This is the heir. Come, let us kill him and have his inheritance'" (Matt. 21:38). Dissatisfied with God's rule, we resolve to make a new world on our own.

Do not imagine this decision to rebel is a happy or fulfilling one. When we view the world as a void without God, we are left to fend for ourselves.

THE EMPTY PROMISES OF IDOLS

Idols lead us to an empty and vain existence. Social media and electronic communication promise a clean and shiny world, but this world is sterile, empty of deep, personal, and meaningful relationships. In fact, we now know that the proliferation of information and connectivity has failed to keep its inherent promise— what was meant to foster better relationships has failed to deliver, and we are far more fractured in our relationships and civility than ever before!

We imagine that our idols serve us; instead, we serve our idols. We become slaves to the images we create. As the psalmist so aptly noted:

> Our God is in the heavens;
>> he does all that he pleases.
>
> Their idols are silver and gold,
>> the work of human hands.
> They have mouths, but do not speak;
>> eyes, but do not see.
> They have ears, but do not hear;
>> noses, but do not smell.
> They have hands, but do not feel;
>> feet, but do not walk;
>> and they do not make a sound in their throat.
> Those who make them become like them,
>> so do all who trust in them.
>
> **PSALM 115:3–8**

Like our lifeless idols, we end up dead in heart and mind, empty in soul and thought. We become programmed to the operations of the media objects we are attached to and end up living a futile, repetitive existence, feeding on the empty images we trust in. To quote author Madeleine Delbrêl:

> *Because you were absent, the whole world seemed to me tiny and ridiculous, and the destiny of man stupid and cruel. A world that was once Christian seems to be in the process of being emptied from within. It first loses God, then the son of God, then everything divine. . . . It is often the surface that is the last thing to collapse.*[5]

DISMANTLING IDOLS

In the Old Testament, idolatry is the presenting sin from which other sins flow. Idolatry is the greatest sin, because loving God is the highest righteousness. As Jesus said, quoting from the Ten Commandments: "Love the Lord your God with all your heart and with all your soul and with all your mind. This is the great and first commandment" (Matt. 22:37–38). While one might suppose that our treatment of others presents the highest good and greatest obligation, it is our treatment of God that is the highest duty and our greatest privilege. God's Law, as listed in the Ten Commandments, reveals a distinct order: the first four commandments describe our duty to God, the last six address our duties to one another, such that being kind to one's neighbor is of no avail if someone is hateful or indifferent toward God. This is why God reserves His greatest indignation and most severe punishments for idolaters.

As we have seen, the Old Testament also reveals *how* the bondage of idols is broken: through humble and repentant prayer! Only then can kings and people identify and destroy the idols, leading to newfound joy, worship, fellowship, and justice. Idols are rendered obsolete and worthy of contempt: "Then you will defile your carved idols overlaid with silver and your gold-plated metal images. You will scatter them as unclean things. You will say to them, 'Be gone!'" (Isa. 30:22).

What is distressing is not so much the proliferation of technology or the succumbing of the culture to its power, but rather how easily Christian believers have given up the fight.

When we take time to converse with God, at the same time we interrupt our dialogue with the world.

The satisfying riches of communicating with God replace our craving for idols and lead to heart-filled repentance. For example, when it comes to digital technology, the more we experience God, the deeper our repentance and renunciation for making this an idol. When the Holy Spirit's sorrow fills our hearts, we know deep within to shut off our cellphones, shut down the television, and shut up the ceaseless noise and pleadings of consumer media.

People who don't know God admit that for most people it is impossible to turn off, restrain, or defeat the power of online media in its various forms. They surrender and complain, "We have lost the battle." Shiny little screens offering endless self-entertainment have won the day.

What is distressing is not so much the proliferation of technology or the succumbing of the culture to its power, but rather how easily Christian believers have given up the fight. We have surrendered the field to what we perceive to be an irresistible army of idols. With condescending glances and dismissive phrases, we refuse to believe the idols of today can be forsaken and destroyed. For this attitude and these words of resignation, God has strong words:

> Your words have been hard against me, says the LORD. But you say, "How have we spoken against you?" You have said, "It is vain to serve God. What is the profit of our keeping his charge or of walking as in mourning before the LORD of hosts?"
> MALACHI 3:13–14

It is understandable if we give up on our culture or even on ourselves. What is treasonous is giving up on God and His power, giving in to unbelief that God can deliver us from the power of modern idols. What are we saying about God when we surrender to these graven images? More to the point, what are we saying about Jesus and about the power of His resurrection when we wave the white flag and give in to a culture restless with greed? To make peace with the world and its idols invites strong rebuke. As Isaiah prophesied:

> In that day the LORD GOD of hosts
>   called for weeping and mourning,
>   for baldness and wearing sackcloth;
> and behold, joy and gladness,
>   killing oxen and slaughtering sheep,
>   eating flesh and drinking wine.
> "Let us eat and drink,
>   for tomorrow we die."
> The LORD of hosts has revealed himself in my ears:
> "Surely this iniquity will not be atoned for you until you die,"
>   says the LORD GOD of hosts.
>
> ISAIAH 22:12–14

This passage is a powerful call to repent of the unbelief that permits us to live and make peace with idols in our lives. To give up on oneself is understandable. To give up on God is to ensure defeat.

Contrary to the naysayers, it is not at all impossible to dismantle the idols of today. Many thousands have found a way to "fight the good fight of the faith" over the enticement of malls and attachment to smartphones and an idolatrous trust of technology. Through consistent prayer believers discern today's idols and their power.

We have experienced this in powerful and practical ways. For example, recently Prayer Current hosted a World Street Experience in downtown Vancouver. Forty-five leaders from around the United States and Canada, as well as four leaders from Moscow and a bishop and his wife from India, met for a five-day prayer summit to unite in prayer for the church and city we met in, as well as the cities they came from. We gathered to experience the power and presence of God as we prayed together, prayer walked the urban core, and engaged in numerous street-level "prayer conversations," in which we asked about the spiritual practices of the city, prayed with people, and shared our own stories about meeting with God in prayer. Our prayers were abundantly answered.

On arriving we asked (not required) that everyone leave their cellphones in their hotel rooms or put them on airplane mode during all sessions and prayer gatherings. Not only did we have 100-percent compliance, no one complained or seemed to mind at all. Our hearts were filled while we experienced God as we prayed together and saw God open hearts as we prayer walked, shared our prayer testimony, and prayed with people on the streets. It was easy to ignore the enticements and demands of digital technology. After we faithfully gathered in earnest and united prayer, we were able to view cellphones as servants, and computers as mere tools.

Christ has not given up His throne, and prayer has not lost its power! Find Christ, and you find freedom. When you learn to revel in the worship of the all-powerful King, you will discover the mall to be a cheap substitute for real treasures. Once the King reigns in your affections, idols will lose their power over you; you can walk through an image-laden mall unmoved by the allure of the idols being offered.

Return to thoughtful praying of the Lord's Prayer and your heart for others will expand toward intercession. Instead of envy and covetousness, your affections will focus on the souls of fellow shoppers, the justice of minimum wage workers, the flourishing of local businesses, the prevention of harm from advertising's exploitation, and the protection of your community's most vulnerable citizens.

Discover God's friendship in prayer, and you will learn to despise self-obsessed trivialities and to forego self-entertainment. Give your moments and hours back to God and others who deserve it and technology will lose its power over your heart. You will be able to turn off news notifications and unplug whenever you judge it helpful. You will have the discipline and power to make technology serve you, rather than you serving it. Prayer will provide you that energy source to strengthen your self-control.

A WAY TO DESTROY THE POWER OF IDOLS

The power of humble and repentant prayer is the only way to break the stranglehold of idols. The idols of the nations surrounding Israel seemed indomitable. Yet in response to earnest, united, repentant prayer, God destroyed the idols one at a time or in a single clean sweep. God reinstated the joy and rest that results from His righteous reign.

So where do *you* begin? The solution is a prayer away. When you reengage with God and fellow believers in prayer and meaningful conversation, you are already loosening the grip of idols. In fact, this is the first and indispensable antidote for breaking the back of your technological obsessions. As soon as you rediscover the joy of prayer and the richness of conversation, you expose and expel the emptiness of virtual communication. The adventure of following God, the soul-filling joy of friendship with fellow believers, and the challenges and hopes contained within our conversations will render idols as unworthy of our time and attention. As we pray, God promises deliverance. We see this in Isaiah 30:19–22:

> He will surely be gracious to you at the sound of your
> cry. As soon as he hears it, he answers you. And though
> the Lord give you the bread of adversity and the water of

affliction, yet your Teacher will not hide himself anymore, but your eyes shall see your Teacher. And your ears shall hear a word behind you, saying, "This is the way, walk in it," when you turn to the right or when you turn to the left. Then you will defile your carved idols overlaid with silver and your gold-plated metal images. You will scatter them as unclean things. You will say to them, "Be gone!"

Enjoy the feast of prayer communion. Get to know one another in prayer (the best way to get to know each other). Early Christians met together every day and were "devoted to prayer." They reaped a harvest of communion and a harvest of growth in evangelism, as we read earlier in Acts 2:42, 44–47.

The greatest reason why we can be confident of victory over the many idols of our hearts and the pervasive and powerful idols of our time is that Christ's ascension presence and power is ours through prayer.

Apart from Christ, we are outgunned and outmanned. In our own poverty and weakness, we have no choice but to surrender and comply with the terms set by the world around us. However, we are never apart from Christ's presence! He dwells above, but we are always with Him (see Eph. 2:6). He dwells above, but He also dwells within (see Col. 1:27). We have not been given a spirit of fear but of power (see 2 Tim. 1:7). Christ already defeated every enemy at the cross and even now rules and reigns with unassailable, majestic confidence. In Him we are more than conquerors (see Rom. 8:37).

We are always with Christ and He with us, yet His deliverance and overcoming are not automatic. Unless and until we pray, we do not experience the needed fullness of Christ's presence and His power. Prayer ignites the ascension power of Christ. That is why the apostle Paul moved from teaching to prayer as he asked God for the Ephesian believers to know, experience, and be inhabited with the very power of the ascended Lord Jesus (see Eph. 1:15–23).

We are in a battle that only Christ can and will finish. We are already winning the war when we gather together on our knees, with hands and voices united in a common cry: "Lord Jesus, fill our hearts with Holy Spirit hope and courage; fuel our prayers and labors by the assurance that this very day, and in this very place, you reign in unassailable sovereign power and that you always honor your promises and answer the prayers of your needy people. Amen!"

Kingdom-Come Prayer Today

1. Looking at the culture around you, what are the idols and images that capture people's imaginations, dreams, and true affections? What do people look to for deliverance in times of need or trouble?

2. In prayerful soul search ask yourself:

   - "Where have I resigned myself to the culture and its idols?"
   - "In what areas do I need to experience freedom from the images and instruments of idolatry in my life?"

   Repent where you have grieved the Holy Spirit through your unbelief.

3. Prayerfully measure your digital usage and dependence on technology. Confess, in specific ways, wherever you have been taken captive in thoughts and habits. In reliance upon our spiritual-battle assets of prayer and power, resolve to consecrate yourself to a holy use of digital technology.

10

HOW EXILES ARE SUSTAINED THROUGH REGENERATING PRAYER

Kingdom advance during captivity

Throughout biblical history, Israel was unable to separate herself from surrounding cultures and became captivated by the idolatry and power of surrounding populations. To set His people free, God sent them into captivity.

His strategy might seem strange. Israel forsook God's law and became an idolatrous nation—so God sent them to a city filled with idols. Israel was enamored with the world's power and prosperity—so God sent them to the most prosperous city the world has ever known. Ancient Babylon was comparable to today's Hong Kong, London, Paris, New York City, or a combination of them all!

It was strange therapy—but it worked. After returning from seventy years of captivity, the nation learned to detest graven images. God raised up leaders who championed Israel's full break with any and all forms of idolatry. When King Nebuchadnezzar erected a massive idol and commanded people to worship it, three heroes defied the king and received swift and horrifying retribution:

> Shadrach, Meshach, and Abednego answered and said to the king, "O Nebuchadnezzar, we have no need to answer you in this matter. If this be so, our God whom we serve is able to deliver us from the burning fiery furnace, and he will deliver us out of your hand, O king. But if not, be it known to you, O king, that we will not serve your gods or worship the golden image that you have set up."
> DANIEL 3:16–18

While the furnace heat ratcheted up to supernova temperatures, one "like a son of the gods" (v. 25) joined them in the ordeal—and not a hair on their heads was singed. Not only so, but King Nebuchadnezzar recognized his folly, reversed course, and required his subjects to acknowledge the God of heaven.

As for Israel's fascination with the power and prestige of surrounding cultures, in order to maintain ethnic and religious separation from all Gentile nations, the Jewish people cultivated an extensive set of boundaries during their exile.

Yet it was God, not Nebuchadnezzar, who sent His people into exile (see Jer. 29:7). He knew the severe humiliation of losing their homeland would bring them back to Him. In this chastening He set them free from idols and from a slavish desire to conform to their surrounding world.

No less than Judah, Christians are exiles in the world today.

Exiles are not only foreigners in the land of their captivity, they are displaced and unwelcome. For example, when I was in grade school, Canada was not multicultural and unwanted immigrants were referred to as "DPs"—displaced persons. It was a term of contempt. Peter was pointing out that as Christians we are not only foreigners in the world, but like Jesus, we are unwelcome—the world will never be home.

As Christian exiles we respect and even love our neighbor. Though we "keep [our] conduct among the Gentiles honorable ... [that] they may see [our] good deeds" (1 Peter 2:12), yet we are to have nothing to do with the idols of the land, nor give God any doubt as to where our loyalties lie. We are citizens of a different country and will never bridge compromising alliances.

Unlike someone who immigrates to a new country (like my parents), whatever indignities or hardships they undergo, an exile's greatest sorrow is that they are away from their homeland. Consider the Jews in Babylon: their deepest yearning was to one day be able to return to the promised land and temple, as they could never be at home in the country of their captivity. While in exile they longed for news from home, and they sent communications to their relatives at every opportunity.

Christians are also away from home. We do our best in this world, carrying out God's commands and commission, but our deepest longing is to be with the Lord and to see Him face to face. In the meantime, we maintain constant communication with our heavenly homeland by reading His living Word and praying at every opportunity.

While in captivity, exiles also find daily comfort as they gather in close fellowship with fellow exiles. In the same way that refugees huddle with their own people, Christians gather with other Christians for their deepest fellowship needs.

Put these two together, constant prayer and daily gathering together, and we have a revolutionary strategy: the more we multiply prayer gatherings, the greater the advance of the kingdom.

We see the power of prayer gatherings in the early church. Virtually every prayer recorded in the book of Acts takes place in corporate prayer gatherings. When God gathers His people in prayer, He has already begun to do a mighty work.

THE EXILES' LIFE OF PRAYER

During their captivity, the Jewish people were separated from the temple and its rituals. They were stripped of their cultural and religious heritage and denied season-marking festivals and temple worship. In essence, they were reduced to the essentials of simple, pure worship of God. Their simplified worship included keeping the Sabbath, reading the Torah, singing the psalms, and saying their prayers. If we are to judge from the biblical narratives in Daniel and Esther, prayer became the chief exercise of faith. In rabbinical teaching and popular piety, prayer took the place of temple sacrifices. While in exile, pious Jews prayed three times each day (see Dan. 6). This daily practice accompanied them for the following centuries, even down to the present day.

We can overlay the narrative of Israel's captivity onto today's cultural and religious milieu, and in so doing observe many parallels. Like captive Judah, we are resident aliens in our cities. We are called "sojourners and exiles" (1 Peter 2:11). In our day, the church of Christ is in constant danger of religious, political, and social captivity. The "world" embodies a domineering cultural, political, and religious force. The powers of our age often oppose the people of God and reject Christ's commands and values. The chasm between the kingdoms of this world and the kingdom of God widens every day.

Christians possess no claim to a promised land or temple. Like exiled Israelites, our worship since the time of Jesus' resurrection has been reduced to the bare essentials: the people of God devote themselves to the apostles' teaching and fellowship, to the breaking of bread and prayers (see Acts 2:42). Our faith connection with God and our experience of His glorious presence are a matter of Word and Spirit, enjoyed through prayer. As John Calvin wrote, "We dig up by prayer the treasures that were pointed out by the Lord's gospel, and which our faith has gazed upon."[1]

PRAYER LESSONS FOR EXILES

Daniel provides a vital lesson for the church in today's idolatrous world. God took Israel to task and to school in Babylon. In head and heart, she would learn five important lessons—lessons we need to learn and remember as well.

Lesson 1: Prayer Rises from Suffering and Adversity

Seventy years of exile and suffering humbled the people of Israel and gave them a thirst for God. Then and now, like nothing else, suffering teaches God's people to pray. God does not willingly afflict anyone (see Lam. 3:33), yet strong medication is often needed to heal the sin-sick soul. Severe adversity leaves a believer weak and needy. Instinctively, he or she cries out for God's help. Those who suffer greatly, when pain and trial is chronic and intense, are humbled and can do little more than groan with the Spirit's help (see Rom. 8:26). This humble sorrow is the prayer God intends, as it brings us home to His love and care.

I have found that weakness can be a gift in disguise. It protects me from pride and vanity. When hurts and trials are deep enough, God leads me into an immediacy of relationship with Him. My only comfort is to rest in that relationship. Through sorrows and trials I learn to be present in His presence. And I find the words of the weeping prophet Jeremiah to be my own:

> My soul continually remembers [my affliction]
>   and is bowed down within me.
> But this I call to mind,
>   and therefore have hope:
>
> The steadfast love of the LORD never ceases;
>   his mercies never come to an end;
> they are new every morning;
>   great is your faithfulness.
> "The LORD is my portion," says my soul,
>   "therefore I will hope in him."
>
> LAMENTATIONS 3:20–24

It is not easy to be an exile, but the fellowship of Christ in these trials is infinitely worth it.

Before the captivity, Israel had become attached to external, material "saviors." They not only worshiped idols, they confused temple rituals with a living relationship with God. They confused the seen world with the unseen. God weaned His people from externals by confining them to the Word and to prayer; by doing so, He led His people into a more profound and unseen faith. He told them, "I will sprinkle clean water on you, and you shall be clean from all your uncleannesses, and from all your idols I will cleanse you. And I will give you a new heart, and a new spirit I will put within you" (Ezek. 36:25–26).

God taught the Jewish people that right worship involves our innermost affections. An inner fire of faith must fuel outward practices. Sacrifices and rituals will not awaken Israel to God's presence and power; only a mighty work of God's Spirit will.

We can apply this lesson of the exiles to the church today. If we measure our success by buildings, staff, and salaries, we are making our home in the world. In contrast, exiles are happy to pitch a tent in the wilderness if it brings them closer to God. In many areas of the world where believers are persecuted, a handful of Christians meeting in a home, a rented space, or a park can enjoy Christ-filled worship, prayer, and fellowship with an intensity and joy we seldom experience. Persecuted Christians have accepted their exile status. They have to keep names and numbers hidden and gather in secrecy. Living in a hostile place, believers are reduced to the unheralded essentials of fellowship and prayer. Jesus commended this way of living:

> The hour is coming, and is now here, when the true worshipers will worship the Father in spirit and truth, for the Father is seeking such people to worship him. God is spirit, and those who worship him must worship in spirit and truth.
>
> JOHN 4:23–24

In one sense, persecuted Christians have an advantage over citizens of a country. They are not looking for their "share of the pie" or a chance to "succeed" or to stand out in comparison with others. This temptation is excluded by their marginal status. In another sense, day by day, majority culture believers have to say no to the status temptations of the surrounding world. This difference between exile and citizen may go a long way to explaining why the church is growing so rapidly in difficult realms.

When we fix our eyes on political leaders to protect the church and to determine the destiny of nations, we have already been taken captive.

Lesson 2: Through Prayer God Protects His People from Political and Cultural Captivity

As illustrated through Daniel's prayer life, God's exiled people took their marching orders from God and not from existing powers. As Daniel prayed, he discerned God's will and plan (see Dan. 2:16–19; 9:3; 10:1). Far from being shaped by the dictates of kings, the political rulers of that day sought Daniel's counsel and wisdom. These world rulers learned that God's kingdom was mighty and His dominion endured from generation to generation (see Dan. 4:3). Daniel prayed for the kingdom of his captors, yet he always prayed that the kingdom of God might be revered and might be revealed.

One of the greatest dangers for God's people in our day is political captivity. As faith in God declines in our secular society, many believers transfer their hopes to governing powers. When God's people become infected by this worldview, they begin to look to political leaders for protection. When we fix our eyes on political leaders to protect the church and to determine the destiny of nations, we have already been taken captive.

In contrast, a life of prayer demonstrates our ultimate assent and affirmation of God's sovereignty in all the affairs of humankind. As we pray, we look to His Word and call upon Him to guard His people, guide the church, and rule the world.

Rather than conform to the powers that be, Christians pray. We pray that rulers, leaders, and culture-shapers in the surrounding world might be blessed, in order that we might cultivate godly lives and effectively proclaim the gospel. Even as we pray for the existing order, as we follow Paul's guidance, we pray for a new order to be revealed:

First of all, then, I urge that supplications, prayers, intercessions, and thanksgivings be made for all people, for kings and all who are in high positions, that we may lead a peaceful and quiet life, godly and dignified in every way. This is good, and it is pleasing in the sight of God our Savior, who desires all people to be saved and to come to the knowledge of the truth.

1 TIMOTHY 2:1–4

Lesson 3: God Rescues His People from Her Enemies

Consider Daniel's supplications and intercessions: he was a one-man prayer revolution. Over the many years of his tenure, at critical junctures, Daniel cried out to God. Each time he prayed, it signaled a dramatic rescue of God's people. Step by step, Daniel's prayers advanced the kingdom cause.

For example, when Daniel united in prayer with his friends, he was ushered into the halls of power. Daniel prayed for wisdom to interpret Nebuchadnezzar's dream. God answered his prayer and gave him the interpretation. The outcome forestalled the execution of all the Babylonian wise men, and Daniel became first among the king's counselors (see Dan. 2). He continued as chief advisor to all three kings of the exile.

Later, Daniel received wisdom to interpret another vision. When King Belshazzar arrogantly chose to drink from the vessels of the temple, he literally saw the writing on the wall. As the king dissolved in terror, Daniel called him to repent and told him that Babylon's world domination was over (see Dan. 5).

Eventually, under the successive Persian Empire, Daniel continued as the chief advisor to the new king. You can imagine how incumbent counselors felt about this. Envious conspirators plotted Daniel's demise. He was ordered to pray to King Darius and no other god. Rather than submit, Daniel flung open his windows and prayed three times a day—and for this he was thrown to the lions. We know the rest: God heard Daniel's prayers from the lion pit, and Daniel was miraculously delivered with not a scratch on him. Moreover, the lions destroyed his conspirators meant for Daniel's demise: "Before they reached the bottom of the den, the lions over-powered them and broke all their bones in pieces" (Dan. 6:24).

Scripture narrative about Daniel's life and prayers provide a powerful example for Christian leaders in the public domain to-day. A supreme loyalty, expressed in utter dependence upon God for answered prayer, is at the beating heart of every leader and every true believer.

Some years later, while the Jewish people remained scattered throughout the empire, God used an ordinary, young Jewish woman to rescue the nation and overthrow Israel's enemies. To save His people, God allowed Esther to become King Xerxes' queen. The king's advisor Haman conspired genocide for God's people, as Pharaoh and later Herod, who slaughtered the inno-cent children, did. Esther interceded on behalf of her people, re-alizing her unique position "for such a time as this" (Est. 4:14). Before daring to petition King Xerxes, she called on God's peo-ple throughout the empire to fast and pray for her. God answered in a mighty way: He rescued the Jewish people and saved them from extinction. God turned the tide of history and reversed the king's pronouncement of doom, as Haman and other enemies were destroyed.

When church or nation is in crisis, we can learn powerful les-sons from Daniel and Esther. Our adversity is God's opportunity. When the forces of this world threaten, we need to fast and pray before we do anything else. When we unite to fast and pray, we strengthen one another in the sure confidence that Almighty God is on the throne and that He appoints and dismantles nations according to His sovereign pleasure. As we pray in the name and sacrificial mediation of Jesus, God will send His thunder and earthquakes to turn the tide of history (see Rev. 8:1–5). Our hope is not in humans. Our help is in the name of the Lord, for He promises: "Call upon me in the day of trouble; I will deliver you, and you shall glorify me" (Ps. 50:15).

Lesson 4: God's People Bless Their Captors in Prayer

God is a missionary God, and He had a missionary purpose for sending Judah into Babylon. He told His people, *Be holy as I am holy,* yet God also intended that they care for those who did not know Him. His forever purpose is that Abraham's children bless all nations: "In your offspring shall all the nations of the earth be blessed" (Gen. 22:18). Even in exile, God's call to pray for the nations abided (see Isa. 56:7).

Even while they were banished, God gave the exiles a prayer directive. He called His people to pray for the city of her captors: "Seek the welfare of the city where I have sent you into exile, and pray to the LORD on its behalf, for in its welfare you will find your welfare" (Jer. 29:7). This promise-filled call to prayer pulsed like a heartbeat throughout the years of exile.

We must understand that God's exiles are His missionaries. And He calls us to bless our society through prayer. As our societies grow more hostile to the gospel, it is easy to "hide our light under a bushel." Apart from prayer, we grow fearful of the surrounding culture. We form enclaves of self-protection and become ingrown. We spend our prayers and energies on self-preservation. Bold mission in a hostile world requires God's presence and power. Apart from united prayer for the advance of the gospel, the prevailing powers will easily overwhelm and drive us back.

Aware of the blatant wickedness and increasing anti-Christian atmosphere today, we might balk at praying for our cities. The words of Jeremiah, however, direct us to a higher calling. If Israel of old was able to pray for the arrogant, idol-ridden city of Babylon, then surely we can intercede in prayer for Toronto, Vancouver, Calgary, New York, Los Angeles, Chicago, Havana, Delhi, Moscow, or any other city in the world. We are called to bless our fellow citizens and seek their well-being, not only because God requires it, but because serving and praying for a healthy city serves the good of God's people and the advancement of the gospel.

Lesson 5: Complete Restoration Comes Through Repentant Prayer

God sent His people to Babylon with a promise of restoration.

> For thus says the LORD: When seventy years are completed for Babylon, I will visit you, and I will fulfill to you my promise and bring you back to this place. For I know the plans I have for you, declares the LORD, plans for welfare and not for evil, to give you a future and a hope. Then you will call upon me and come and pray to me, and I will hear you. You will seek me and find me, when you seek me with all your heart.
> JEREMIAH 29:10–13

Daniel recalled Jeremiah's promise and represented the nation in a repentant plea for God to forgive and restore this people to the promised land. Daniel consecrated himself to intercession. A passionate and urgent prayer of repentance followed.

> We have sinned and done wrong and acted wickedly. . . . We have not listened. . . . To us, O LORD, belongs open shame. . . . We have not entreated the favor of the LORD our God.
> DANIEL 9:5–6, 8, 13

Daniel's prayer culminated in a mighty plea (vv. 4–19): "O LORD, forgive. O LORD, pay attention and act. Delay not, for your own sake."

God heard Daniel's prayer and brought Israel home.

Increasingly, believers today feel captive to the surrounding culture. Christians not only face general disdain for their beliefs and practices, but leaders in government, education, and the courts legislate laws that are anti-biblical and entirely averse to the cause of Christ. A Christian response goes far beyond the ballot box. Like Daniel, we need to intercede and repent on behalf of the church and nation. We need to follow God's command from 2 Chronicles 7:14—to humble ourselves, pray, seek God's face, and turn from our wicked ways, so that the Lord will hear and forgive and heal.

Like Daniel, each child of Christ is "highly favored" and can grow mighty in prayer. We too can intercede for the church and nation. Realizing how God used Daniel's prayers to restore and revive Israel, why would we not also unite in earnest and concerted prayer?

THE LIFE OF AN EXILE IS A LIFE OF PRAYER

Like the exiles of Daniel's day, we have no promised land or holy city. We, too, are aliens and sojourners with no fixed address. Our true residence is in heaven (see Heb. 13:14). Our worship is not a matter of outward temple or rituals; our life in this world is sustained by prayer and Scripture.

Yet perhaps more than any other time in recent history, the events of exile and captivity apply to us. As "exile Christians," we are never at peace with the present world order. Like righteous Lot, we are greatly distressed by the sensual conduct of the wicked (see 2 Peter 2:7) and have made a decisive break with the world around us.

At the same time, Christians are a blessing to those around them. Wherever we look in the needy parts of our country—the mean streets of the inner city, on Indian reservations, among refugees and immigrants—wherever people are lonely, hungry, poverty stricken or marginalized, we see God's people hard at work praying and serving those in need. The world will always complain about Christians, but woe to the world if Christians were to be removed!

While Christians serve, they pray, crying out night and day on behalf of the church and for the land of their exile. As they pray, believers have their hopes fixed on God. Burning jealousy for Christ's honor fills them with a broad generosity; out of a renewed heart they yearn and pray for the ingathering of many.

The conquering force of prayer over the powers of the city is proven again and again in Scripture and in history. As the church unites in earnest prayer, she remains true to her Lord. Moreover, like salt and leaven, she permeates the culture, politics, and religious life of her captors. The gates of our cities open in answer to prayers, and God's people enter in and bless their neighbors (see Acts 12:10).

EMBRACING OUR EXILE STATUS

God wants us to embrace our exile status. The alternative would be to make our home in this world and deny our eternal birthplace. But James reminds us, "Friendship with the world is enmity with God" (James 4:4). We don't expect fair treatment from the world. We are used to being maligned as fundamentalists, even as dangerous. It is an honor to be maligned for the cause of Christ (see Acts 5:41). Increasingly, we face different forms of discrimination, hostility, and repression. We do not find justice for God's people at the polls or law courts. Justice and righteousness will visit the land when we gather in united and earnest prayer.

If you are an exile, you are not a citizen. You have no vote when it comes to your rights as a believer. You cannot argue or appeal to the powers that be. If the government or people turn against you, you have no earthly weapons to defend yourself. God has given you another kind of power—as powerful and invincible as Christ Himself. God has given you prayer. Recall how Jewish exiles turned to prayer again and again and in every desperate situation. With mighty miracles, God answered the united prayers of His people, overturning the plans of wicked leaders and advancing the cause of His kingdom. Daniel called others to pray; Shadrach, Meshach, and Abednego united in prayer; and Esther called the nation to prayer. The call of an exile is to gather with fellow believers in prayer. The outcome will be a prayer revolution.

Kingdom-Come Prayer Today

1. In what ways are believers today threatened by political, religious, and cultural captivity? In what ways have you been threatened? Where have we compromised and failed to be separate from the surrounding culture and thus compromised our calling?

2. How can we bless the city of our exile? In what ways can you intercede for her well-being and prosperity?

Cuban Christians (2017)

Cuban Christians are exiles in both biblical and practical ways. In Cuba, believers are not part of the political process. They are not included in civic discourse. The church is separate from the halls of power. Yet the church has a palpable vibrancy and love. Cubans love to pray, and they love to serve those in need. Christians do not complain about the government; instead, they pray for the government. They do not hide from the surrounding city; rather, they step out and serve the people in countless ways. Many churches hold sports camps for children and youth. When hurricanes hit, they set up food stations. In Old Havana, Christians are the ones repairing the crumbling facades of their streets. They serve meals to the elderly and disabled. Where and when they can, they preach the Good News. Everyday believers are faithful in sharing the gospel, and the Cuban people are attracted to the church. Though official numbers are not available, universal agreement exists that the church is experiencing revival.[2] Although the church lies on the margins of society, it is a city within the city. It is a countercultural source of hope in a communist country.

When our Prayer Current team was in Cuba in 2017, we held three full days of prayer evangelism workshops in three different cities. In downtown Havana, less than 350 feet from the capital building, we divided into pairs and headed to Fraternity Park; each pair had between two and four prayer-evangelism conversations. We held a conversation with Brian, the owner of an amulet shop, who grew interested as we talked and prayed for him. Then we chatted with Isabel, a desperately lonely woman whose son was in prison in America. Next we talked with Ryan, who was eager to get a Bible. We have good hopes for his salvation.

Afterward, we gathered as a group under the shadow of the national legislature. In a large circle, we held hands, shared testimonies, sang, and prayed for the country. Nearby, a woman read tarot cards for a few pesos, and three of our team members peeled off to share the gospel with her. After an energetic discussion, the woman removed her magic beads and asked to receive a Bible.

While the military patrolled the capital building, these simple believers huddled together and embraced their exile status. Armed only with prayer and love for their fellow countrymen, they were part of a revolution the communists never dreamed of.

HOW A CHURCH IS REVIVED AND A CITY IS RENEWED THROUGH PRAYER

A new song rises from united prayer

What will it look like when a prayer revolution comes to pass? We will be able to see it, hear it, and feel it in space and time, here and now. When His kingdom comes, His good will shall be done on this very earth as in heaven.

In certain hope, lift your gaze to a future horizon; observe when church and civic leaders come together to plan the rebuilding of a city, recruiting church members and willing citizens to join in. Contemplate how it will feel when the mean streets of sin and sorrow become places of safety, play, and laughter for children, lined with benches where mothers and elderly sit together, looking on the fun with faces stretched with happiness. Or picture the wild streets where young people wander through piercing and tattoo parlors and see beyond to one day those places becoming gathering spots of free and open conversation about truth, beauty, and meaning. With eyes of faith, foresee a future where the tidy avenues of the well-to-do, suppressed by barren indulgence and crippling loneliness, come alive with hope for the future. Hear the joyous songs rising from the people of God when they forsake their cloistered gatherings and own their community as a parish, all the while the surrounding neighbors go in and out at will, knowing they will be welcomed and cared for. You can announce the coming day to everyone: these dreams will become reality as God brings His prayer revolution to pass.

The books of Ezra and Nehemiah paint this picture in panoramic history and splendid detail. (The prophetic books of Haggai and Zechariah provide essential background.) A century of church and civic renewal comes together at the end in Nehemiah 12. Priests, rulers, and people have joined together, laboring to complete building the temple and city walls, and it is time to celebrate this work of God. Hand in hand, with voices united, they circle the city and congregate in the sanctuary precincts. The courts are filled with rejoicing, and the city joins the song: "The two choirs that gave thanks then took their places in the house of God. . . . And on that day they offered great sacrifices, rejoicing because God had given them great joy. The women and children also rejoiced. The sound of rejoicing in Jerusalem could be heard far away" (Neh. 12:40, 43 NIV).

This is revival in its fullness: a revived church and a renewed city. Let's survey the history to see how this glorious revolution came to pass and what it means for us as well.

CHURCH REVIVAL AND CITY RENEWAL TAKE TIME

What does a prayer revolution look like? We maintain that the fullness of God's kingdom purpose is not only for the people of

God to be awakened to powerful worship and deep fellowship, but also through her prayers and ministrations, surrounding cities are rebuilt and the nation flourishes.

The Bible provides an extensive survey of this very reality in the narrative of the century from the return of the exiles to the "church and city" celebration of Nehemiah 12. A prayerful reading of Ezra, Nehemiah, Zechariah, Haggai, and Malachi yields a profound description of how a prayer revolution comes to pass, and how long it can take before it bears lasting fruit.

We notice from chapters 5 and 8 that church awakenings and revivals can happen suddenly, with Pentecost explosiveness. However, it takes significantly longer for the salt and leaven to penetrate and transform the surrounding society and its culture. In the case of the returning exiles, the fullness of this revolution takes nearly one hundred years and involves a series of awakenings.

It begins with praying for God's kingdom to come, asking for the awakening of the church, as well as the flourishing of the city in which she dwells, as God commanded: "Seek the welfare of the city where I have sent you into exile . . . for in its welfare you will find your welfare" (Jer. 29:7).

The Old Testament books of Ezra and Nehemiah reveal how individual and congregational prayers at critical junctures over almost a hundred years called down the Spirit's power and brought both revival in the church and healing of the city.

However, even with the prayers of the faithful, holistic kingdom advance was not realized in a few years, or even decades. In the Old Testament accounts, it took more than ninety years to arrive at the union of church and city. Returning exiles laid the foundation of the temple in 537 BC; later generations completed rebuilding the city walls in 445 BC. In other words, it took almost a century for the temple and city to come together. Starts and stops, encouraging times and discouraging times marked the years leading to Jerusalem's great awakening. The historical chart below indicates the chronology.[1]

CHRONOLOGY OF EZRA-NEHEMIAH	YEAR
General period of captivity	605–536 BC
Leading Judean citizens deported, including Daniel and Ezekiel	605, 597, 586
Nebuchadnezzer of Babylon conquers Judah	586
Cyrus of Persia decrees return of the Jews	538
Return of 49,897 from Babylon to Jerusalem	536
Altar rebuilt, sacrifice offered in seventh month	536
Temple rebuilding begun, but stopped	535
Economic and political struggle	535–520
Ministry of Haggai	520
Ministry of Zechariah	520–515
Temple completed	515
Ahasuerus becomes king of Persia	486
Artaxerxes I becomes king of Persia	464
Return of Ezra to Jerusalem	458
Nehemiah rebuilt the walls	445

This example teaches us that before great fires can burn, smaller fires need to be lit.

I bought some poplar wood recently. When I tried to light it, I found it was wet, which meant it was hard to light. At first I lit the fresh kindling and cardboard under the logs. As soon as the kindling was exhausted, the fire went out. I repeated the process, adding more kindling and cardboard and the flames burned a little brighter and longer. After two more tries, the wet wood was finally dry and hot enough to burst into a lasting fire. After a while, even wet wood could be added, and the fire blazed even brighter.

When church and city are in serious decline, as in the West

today, it is like lighting wet wood. We are at the early stages of church revival and urban renewal, but the wood is wet. We must put fresh kindling under the logs and light it again and again until the fire blazes on its own.

SEVERAL MINI REVIVALS MAY BE NEEDED TO RESULT IN A GREAT REVIVAL

There were lesser revivals before the great celebration of Nehemiah. After the temple foundations were set in place in 537 BC, the people held a mini-celebration: "When the builders laid the foundation of the temple of the LORD . . . all the people shouted with a great shout when they praised the LORD" (Ezra 3:10–11).

However, this modest beginning was short-lived. The returning exiles caved under pressure from the surrounding foreigners and halted construction of the temple. Both priests and people left the city and drifted back to their homes.

After a decade of inactivity, the prophet Haggai awakened the people's conscience: "Is it a time for you yourselves to be living in your paneled houses, while this house remains a ruin?" (Hag. 1:4 NIV). Finally, two decades after starting the project, the people completed rebuilding the temple (see Ezra 6:14).

With temple service restored, the community marked the achievement: "The people of Israel—the priests, the Levites and the rest of the exiles—celebrated the dedication of the house of God with joy" (Ezra 6:16 NIV).

However, this brief revival also subsided, and a sixty-year gap occurred in the narrative. Jerusalem entered into yet another period of religious and social decline. The people deserted the temple service and abandoned city precincts; the walls of the city remained in ruins.

In our time and place, we can see signs that we are only in the early stages of church revival and urban renewal. Still, until the Lord grants a mighty awakening, we faithfully and patiently pray, work and wait for the leaven to do its work. As we consider the immensity of the task and the slow progress of change, it is easy to grow weary. We find that hearts can be cold and doors closed. But we stay committed to pray for vigilance. As Paul wrote, "[We pray that you will be] strengthened with all power, according to his glorious might, for all endurance and perseverance with joy" (Col. 1:11). We must try be careful that we don't "despise the day of small things" (Zech. 4:10).

The great missionary and explorer to Africa, David Livingstone, provides a great example of patient endurance. He never lived to see the fruit of his labors. Some questioned why he bothered to hike some 29,000 arduous miles through jungles and deserts to explore and map Africa. Livingstone's stirring words explain his reasoning:

> Missionaries in the midst of masses of heathenism seem like voices crying in the wilderness . . . future missionaries will see conversions follow every sermon. We prepare the way for them. May they not forget the pioneers who worked in the thick gloom with few rays to cheer, except such as flow from faith in God's promises! We work for a glorious future which we are not destined to see. . . . We are only morning stars shining in the dark, but the glorious morn will break.[2]

Today, more than a century later, many of Africa's millions are turning to Christ.

Because we too may not see great numbers of conversions in the short term, we cannot afford to rest our hopes on the present results of our labors. Rather, when the going gets tough, we must be "looking to Jesus, the founder and perfecter of our faith, who for the joy that was set before him endured the cross, despising the shame, and is seated at the right hand of the throne of God" (Heb. 12:2). When we pray with the eyes of faith, we see Jesus as He is now, and we immediately participate in the victory of His death and the power of His ascension glory. As Paul stated, "You have been filled in him, who is the head of all rule and authority" (Col. 2:10). This is the greatest encouragement of all. The psalmist painted a poignant picture of the great reward following years of toil: "Those who sow in tears shall reap with shouts of joy! He who goes out weeping, bearing the seed for sowing, shall come home with shouts of joy, bringing his sheaves with him" (Ps. 126:5–6).

Let's look deeper into the books of Ezra and Nehemiah to get a better sense of what renewal looks like, why we need to be faithful and patient as we pray, and what lessons we can apply to our own prayer revolution as we trust that our work will not be in vain.

It is not only impossible for the city to flourish if the church lies in ruins, God's plan for the church will not be complete as long as the city is in decline.

THE FUTURE OF THE CHURCH IS CONNECTED TO THE FUTURE OF THE CITY

In post-exile Jerusalem one reason the temple was neglected was because its ongoing service depended on the safety a strong and secure city could provide. As long as the city walls laid in ruin, the temple remained unprotected. Clearly, the fate of the temple was tied to the fate of the city.

In many ways, the fate of the church is still tied to the fate of the cities we live in. It is not only impossible for the city to flourish if the church lies in ruins, God's plan for the church will not be complete as long as the city is in decline. The great vision of God is for both church and city to be united and to be in harmony. (See the next chapter and the explanation of Rev. 21).

In many cities, the church is weakened because, metaphorically, the walls of our cities are weak and the gates broken. We have diced our neighborhoods with highways. We scatter our population with urban sprawl. Because we live, work, and play in different places, we seldom cross paths with one another, and we have less time to invest in community life. City life becomes fragmented and its citizens are exhausted by the increasing demands. Our frenzied lifestyle works against forming strong social bonds and church fellowships. On a typical Sunday, while non-Christians might gather in homes, often to watch a sporting event, Christians drive past the homes in that very community to congregate with other Christians. After church, non-Christians and Christians alike head home, close their garage doors, and retreat to their privacy. During the week, adjoining neighbors drive, or take public transportation, to various jobs and activities miles apart from their neighbor. And many days, the church building lies empty, except for staff meetings and perhaps a gathering or two during the week. It simply takes a lot of effort to bring people together.

Contrast this with Cuba, for example, where few people have cars or even motorcycles. Public transportation is horse-drawn carts or bicycles, so that many Cubans spend most of their time in their local community and walk from place to place. They often cross paths with neighbors, and are able to meet in homes and public places several times a week. Close-knit house churches result. This is fertile soil for community growth and outreach. People view the church building or house church as a friendly gathering place. A welcoming house church fellowship or Sunday morning service readily and quickly embraces those who are lonely or in need. Newcomers love it, and no one is in a hurry to jump in a car and get home for lunch or to watch a football game.

Yes, we have a city problem, but we also have a church problem. The two are intertwined. Both need to succeed, and we must pray for both.

GOD SENDS THE RIGHT PEOPLE TO BRING RENEWAL

Returning to the biblical history, in 458 BC, nearly sixty years after the temple's first rebuilding, a fiery priest named Ezra arrived in Jerusalem. He found the temple abandoned and the city walls in ruins. Unapologetically, Ezra called a fast for repentance. Out of his passionate prayer a new awakening arose:

> I . . . fell upon my knees and spread out my hands to the LORD my God, saying:
> "O my God, I am ashamed and blush to lift my face to you, my God, for our iniquities have risen higher than our heads, and our guilt has mounted up to the heavens. . . . But now for a brief moment favor has been shown by the LORD our God . . . that our God may brighten our eyes and grant us a little reviving in our slavery."
> EZRA 9:5–6, 8

God honored the fast, answered Ezra's prayer, and revived the hopes of the people. However, this revival was also short-lived: fourteen years of inactivity followed, and once again temple service was neglected and the city abandoned.

But revival in its fullness did not happen until God sent a city-builder to Jerusalem. While Ezra performed the priestly work, God used Nehemiah to implement the city building—the construction of walls and gates, and renewal of hearts for the mission.

In 445 BC, when Nehemiah heard that the walls of Jerusalem lay in ruins, he fasted and prayed for four months, from Chislev (December) to Nissan (April). Like Ezra, in deep shame and humiliation, Nehemiah confessed his own sin and the wickedness of his people:

> "O LORD God of heaven, the great and awesome God who keeps covenant and steadfast love with those who love him and keep his commandments, let your ear be attentive and your eyes open, to hear the prayer of your servant that I now pray before you day and night for the people of Israel your servants, confessing the sins of the people of Israel, which we have sinned against you. Even I and my father's house have sinned. . . . Remember the word that you commanded your servant Moses, saying, 'If you are unfaithful, I will scatter you among the peoples, but if you return to me . . . I will gather them and bring them to the place that I have chosen, to make my name dwell there.' . . . O Lord, let your ear be attentive to the prayer of your servant, and to the prayer of your servants who delight to fear your name, and give success to your servant today, and grant him mercy in the sight of this man."
>
> NEHEMIAH 1:5–6, 8–9, 11

Nehemiah's prayer bore fruit. King Artaxerxes intervened for the exiles to return and sent Nehemiah to Jerusalem to rebuild the city walls.

Upon his arrival, before meeting with anyone, Nehemiah took a prayer walk. He circled the city to assess its broken walls and to see things from God's perspective (see Neh. 2:13).

In our church and ministry life, we have found that "seeing the city with God's eyes" is one of the chief blessings coming out of our many prayer walks in Vancouver. As we circumnavigate our neighborhoods in prayer, we note signs of decay and signs of renewal. We pray "onsite with insight." Every time we head out to pray, the Spirit of Christ grants us a growing awareness of God's viewpoint and the baseline realities of the city. We are able to discern a blueprint, which guides our strategic outreach.

In the same way, Nehemiah's prayer walk led to a prophetic call to action:

> "You see the trouble we are in, how Jerusalem lies in ruins with its gates burned. Come, let us build the wall of Jerusalem, that we may no longer suffer derision." And I told them of the hand of my God that had been upon me for good, and also of the words that the king had spoken to me. And they said, "Let us rise up and build."
> NEHEMIAH 2:17–18

God's people set to work and repaired the walls in just fifty-two days. Once they hung the bronze gates of the city in place, Jerusalem was able to provide safety for its inhabitants and protection for the temple. After ninety-three years of revival and decline, the temple and the city were finally in harmony.

If we ever hope to rebuild the church and city, we must heed the crucial lesson here. Revival is a team sport: not only do we need pastors, but often city-builders will lead the charge. At the right time, God will raise up an explorer like David Livingstone or a champion of the oppressed like William Wilberforce to lead the advance of the kingdom. When that happens, we who are clergy not only need to get out of the way, we need to make a way for these heroes to lead us to a new day.

A CELEBRATION OF COSMIC PROPORTION ENSUES

Once the temple was restored, and priests and Levites mustered, and the city walls repaired, and the bronze gates of the city hung, it was time to celebrate! Priests, rulers, and people came together to keep the Feast of Booths and "there was very great rejoicing" (Neh. 8:17).

At the end of the feast, Ezra led the people in a full day of Scripture reading and prayer. The people raised a heartfelt confession of sin and made a covenant with God to restore temple worship and to repopulate the city (see Neh. 11:1–2).

This happy peace, between temple and city, won by a priest and a city-builder, led to a thanksgiving celebration of cosmic proportions. Worshiping priests and festal choirs paraded around the three-kilometer parapet that encircled the city. Filling out the grand assembly were forty thousand people who crowded the temple courts.

Two choirs met together atop the wall overlooking the temple. They formed an orchestral assembly of five hundred worshipers. Men and women singers lifted their songs until tears covered their faces. Two hundred priests and Levites blew the trumpet-like shofar. Others played musical instruments to praise God with all their might. Many thousands of people filling the temple courts joined in and sang the Great Hallel:

> Praise the LORD.
>
> Praise the LORD, you his servants;
>> praise the name of the LORD.
> Let the name of the LORD be praised,
>> both now and forevermore.
> From the rising of the sun to the place where it sets,
>> the name of the LORD is to be praised.

PSALM 113:1–3 NIV

This is what the prophets, priests, kings, and people had been foretelling, working, and waiting for. At long last, the city and the sanctuary were in harmony: the renewed city protecting the temple, while temple worship brought life and joy to the city. The vision and promises of the prophets had come to pass: "Build my house, so that I may take pleasure in it and be honored" (Hag. 1:8 NIV).

This has always been God's plan and promise: a city protecting the church and a church pulsing with the Spirit, bringing laughter and joy to the heart of the city. This is the revolution of all revolutions. Even today, this grand enterprise is what Jesus is about. In ascension power and authority, He is saving many, growing and building His church. At the same time our King is sending each of us, and all of us together, to rebuild the city. Every step of the way is initiated and accompanied by our prayers for the church and city.

THIS HISTORY OF REVIVAL CONTAINS LESSONS FOR TODAY

We can make several applications to our present situation.

First, revival in its fullness requires time. Short-term strategies promising church revival and urban renewal are unrealistic and naive. We must measure urban mission in decades, not years. Renovation always takes longer than building from scratch. When a new building replaces an older one, existing walls need to tumble, and the rubble will need to be cleared away before new foundations can be laid. Much time and labor is required at the renovation stage, and this hard work will remain hidden and unheralded. When it comes time to build a tall building on this ground, clearing the old away takes time. Not only so, but digging the hole afterwards, shoring the walls, and pouring the foundations take many months. The taller the structure, the more work is unseen. Once the below-the-ground work is finished, in a matter of weeks, a building rises to meet the sky. All previous labor is easily forgotten.

Today we are in the renovation and groundwork stage. It is not helpful to pretend or prophesy that towers of change will immediately soar to the sky. Our labor is always a matter of faith as we look forward to the city that only God can build (see Heb. 11:10).

Second, church and city often exist in tension. In our day, the church has suffered neglect, and the spiritual and moral walls of the city are in ruins. It helps to know that this is not the first time the church has had to face a world in decay. David wrote prophetically of what we are seeing in our time: "I see violence and strife in the city. Day and night they go around it on its walls, and iniquity and trouble are within it; ruin is in its midst; oppression and fraud do not depart from its marketplace" (Ps. 55:9–11).

For the most part, in our time the church and the city seem far removed from each other. Sunday churchgoing remains disconnected from city life. The church lies on the periphery. While church attendance declines, the surrounding urban culture becomes increasingly cynical and gospel-resistant. God's people always feel the tension and opposition, and are often tempted to withdraw or return cynicism with cynicism.

Those who live in our secular cities will see glimmers of promise, but will also experience opposition, seen and unseen, both inside and outside the walls to slow and even halt the progress. The surrounding atmosphere of unbelief will dampen our hopes. In the church, a rising tide of compromise and even apostasy threatens to undo much of the good already done. As the angel exhorted, "Here is a call for the endurance of the saints" (Rev. 14:12).

To each of the seven churches of Asia Minor, Jesus warned and promised that only "the one who conquers [that perseveres to the end]" will be part of His eternal city (see Rev. 2–3).

Third, as we unite in prayer, God will raise up leaders for the work. Consider how God conscripted mighty kings—Cyrus, Darius, and Artaxerxes—to support the temple project. He sent prophets such as Haggai, Zechariah, and Malachi to encourage the people to rebuild the temple and to reignite dying embers of revival. God raised up godly leaders of courage—temple-builders like Zerubbabel, preachers like Ezra, and city-builders like Nehemiah. Time and again, the priests, the Levites, and the people offered themselves in holy array and service to God's kingdom purposes.

As we unite to pray, we can expect the same result—that God will conscript rulers, send prophets, raise up builders, and enable workers to rebuild His house. If we wholeheartedly give ourselves to prayer, we will slowly but certainly witness the harmony God brings between the church and city. We need prophets and preachers like Haggai and Zechariah to call us to repentance. We need civic leaders who are fed by God's vision. We need God to raise up temple-builders like Ezra and city-builders like Nehemiah.

Jesus looked at the city and called us to pray to the Lord of the harvest for harvest workers (see Luke 10:2). In response, we need to pray for God to raise up the larger army of evangelists. These people can be from any location or any sector of society. For example, as I write this, a young lawyer in Winnipeg has gathered eight lawyers to pray each month for the judiciary. In my province, a strong and gifted woman leader of a faith-based public housing corporation trains her site and building leaders how to lead their teams in prayer and to pray for their guests. Doubtless God has placed leaders of His revolution in places of government, education, business, arts, entertainment, industry, and judiciary. Pray for God to raise up many more, for these people to be bold in witness, to be salt and leaven in deeds of justice and mercy.

Fourth, Christ is the one who ultimately brings church and city together in harmony. The prophets, priests, and kings who rebuilt the city and the temple in Jerusalem were a composite picture of Jesus—the final prophet, the perfect priest, and the everlasting king—who builds, cleanses, and inhabits His temple. As Mark reminds us, "We heard him say, 'I will destroy this temple that is made with hands, and in three days I will build another, not made with hands'" (Mark 14:58).

At the same time, even now, Jesus is building an eternal city whose architect and builder is God (Heb. 11:10). He is preparing the New Jerusalem, the perfect temple-city (Rev. 21). This is not only an "end-time" vision. Those who believe in Jesus embody a living, breathing temple-city as we await the eternal, unshakable kingdom to come:

> You yourselves like living stones are being built up as a spiritual house, to be a holy priesthood, to offer spiritual sacrifices acceptable to God through Jesus Christ. . . . But you are a chosen race, a royal priesthood, a holy nation, a people for his own possession, that you may proclaim the excellencies of him who called you out of darkness into his marvelous light.
>
> **1 PETER 2:5, 9**

God places a challenge and call before every Christian: join the world or join the revolution. It is your choice. Spend and expend your life to experience the prevalent emptiness of flesh and fashion or throw all your heart, labors, and prayers, enlisting with King Jesus, to experience the surpassing power and joy of His presence, as He carries out His grand plan of rebuilding the church and city.

CHRISTIANS ARE CALLED TO BE CHURCH-BUILDERS AND CITY-BUILDERS

For believers, our kingdom calling is to revive the church and renew the city. To revive the church, we unite in prayer and beseech the Spirit's power. We become a house of prayer for the nations (see Isa. 56:7). We serve God's people with generous joy and gracious self-giving. To rebuild the city, we first acknowledge the biblical mandate to be city-builders. We are called to dwell in the city, to pray for the city, to proclaim Christ to the city, to repair the city, and to fill the city with joy and justice. As Isaiah proclaimed:

> If you spend yourselves in behalf of the hungry
>> and satisfy the needs of the oppressed,
> then your light will rise in the darkness,
>> and your night will become like the noonday. . . .
> Your people will rebuild the ancient ruins
>> and will raise up the age-old foundations;
> you will be called Repairer of Broken Walls,
>> Restorer of Streets with Dwellings.
>
> ISAIAH 58:10, 12 NIV

God provides the blueprint. It is up to us to build the show-home that reveals what, one day, the new neighborhood will be like.

Those who pray the promises of God can rest in His timing and truth: no matter how long it takes, revival will come in response to prayer. It is not a matter of if; it is a matter of when.

In Canada today, new churches are being established in the heart of many cities and on the campuses of many universities. Alpha Canada's outreach to youth is spreading to hundreds of high schools and they are reaching more than sixty prisons across the country. Courageous Christians minister to new immigrants and serve in destitute neighborhoods. This same bold and creative outreach is happening in the United States. At the core of these praying churches is a growing awareness of the happy partnership between preaching Christ and practicing justice and kindness in the public square.

We will know that our prayers are bearing fruit when increasing numbers of believers gather in homes to pray and engage in congregational days of prayer and fasting and in prayer walks around their neighborhoods.

We will know God is answering our prayers and blessing our labors when church doors are open to those who seek to know God—people from every nation can stream in and learn His glorious way of salvation.

In the meantime, we patiently wait and pray for the day when the city walls will be in place to protect the sanctuary. What we pray for is what we become. After deep foundations are laid, the church will begin to soar upward. Homes will be inhabited and streets filled with the joyous sounds of children at play. Community life will flourish; justice and truth will be the hallmarks of city life. One day, not next week or next year, but perhaps soon if Christ pleases, a pure and joyous song will ascend from the church to God and fill the city with joy! With Christ guarding, guiding, and bringing to pass this revolution, all of our labors and prayers are filled with expectant hope.

Kingdom-Come Prayer Today

1. Get to know your city or community at the ground level. Prayer walking the community is a great way to see things from God's perspective. Like Nehemiah, circle the downtown of your city and survey the state of its "walls." Give thanks for churches and missions that are seeking to serve God and the community. Pray for centers of influence—media, arts, education, government, and industry.

2. Pray that God will give you His eyes to see and His heart to care. Seek to gain Christ's compassion and "harvest eyes" for your neighborhood (see Matt. 9:37–38).

Cuba (1940–Present)

Reminiscent of Jerusalem's post-exilic period of decline is the recent history of Cuba. In the late 1950s not all Christians were opposed to Castro's communist revolution, yet after the communists came to power, the church suffered wide persecution. Believers went into hiding, and some were imprisoned. The gates of the country closed to the voices of its Christian citizens, as well as to foreign Christian missionaries.

Yet God has been raising up another city within the city. Since 1990 the church of Christ has rapidly grown within Cuba. Believers preach boldly, pray urgently, and worship vibrantly. In keeping with their love of culture and the arts, one congregation spends weeks repairing old buildings in the surrounding neighborhood. A young couple began an outreach ministry to the arts community, hoping to establish a creative congregation in the city center. Recently, police reported to one pastor that the neighborhood's crime rate has declined 40 percent since that church's outreach began.

One Christian group in Cuba, poised to split in the 1990s over issues of liberty and legalism, stayed together and now comprises two hundred churches and more than a thousand house churches. In recent years, its leaders have introduced gospel renewal and kingdom prayer, and the group has established seven training centers in seven leading cities and has trained around eight thousand pastors and lay pastors.

The testimony of a Cuban church leader demonstrates how prayer unites church and city: "Cubans love art. Cuban artists paint the thoughts they are not free to express in words. Each week we host art evenings in the church so that local artists can gather to sip coffee and to display and discuss their art." The pastor reports that eight house churches were started and that thirty artists came to faith in Christ in the first five years of this ministry. He said, "When we came to Hoguin, our launch team went to a hilltop overlooking the city and circled in prayer. We not only prayed to start new churches, we prayed kingdom prayers and asked God to help us reach and bless the whole city."

Christians in Cuba practice sacrificial giving. Though many wait in long lines for simple bread and rice, and may go several days without meat or vegetables, these believers are generous in sharing all they have with everyone. They set up distribution centers to help their neighbors in time of need. Increasingly, many of their fellow citizens view the church as the generous provider of social welfare. Of course, they deny it by giving all the thanks to Christ.

PRAYING THE SPIRIT'S VISION

"Lord, revive Your people and heal our land"

A revolution of prayer cries out for an ultimate vision to ignite it. With a few good clear, measurable, and attainable goals, we can make progress. But what fuels real revolution is having a compelling and cosmic picture of what the world will one day look like.

Every revolution requires this. Conquerors wage war holding onto the dream of a day when all peoples are in subjection to their rule; communists rework the world because they imagine a future world of social equality; nature activists envision a day of ecological harmony; pacifists work for world peace and an end to war; new-agers proselytize the world in the belief that ignorance will one day dissolve into a divine consciousness; feminists never cease advocating for women in every sector of society and country of the world, believing it is just and right for women to be treated equally with men. Wherever the world is being turned upside down, whether by Christians or non-Christians, behind all the labor, sacrifice, and proselytizing lies a compelling vision that followers believe and dedicate their lives to.

All the prayers, evangelism, and deeds of justice and mercy in a Christian revolution (awakening or revival) are also fueled by a vision. The Christian's picture of final destiny is unique in striking ways. First, the vision is revealed, not imagined. It is given by God in Scripture and is not a product of human genius. Second, this promise-filled picture is comprehensive of every dream, imagination, or hope ever to come into the heart and mind of people. God promises reconciliation of all things—church, city, and the rest of creation—and "things in heaven and things on earth" (Eph. 1:10) will soon unite in glorious splendor and everlasting harmony. Third, this foretold destiny is not humans' attainment; the vision given us is not only wished for, it is guaranteed by almighty God.

> **We become what we pray, so the more we pray into these visions, the more we experience their reality and live them out.**

This is what we cling to as we pursue our prayer revolution. But what is this vision that fuels us?

To discover it, we turn once again to Scripture in which the prophets offer dramatic illustrations and striking metaphors supplied by the Spirit. The life and flow of the coming kingdom are portrayed in majestic visions of hope. Because these visions are God's promises, not just wishes, they will certainly come to pass. The more we prayerfully dive into them, the more our present thoughts and actions are motivated and carried forward in unshakeable hope. We become what we pray, so the more we pray into these visions, the more we experience their reality and live them out.

This is what happened with the people throughout the Bible.

Isaiah, Zechariah, Ezekiel, and the grand finale in Revelation offer us prominent images and a clear vision of Holy Spirit revival. Prayer, temple, and city motifs repeat throughout. Even now, from temple and city flows a vast and deep river of salvation and healing, increasing in depth and current, until humankind's story arrives at its glorious fulfillment.

Prayer revolutions are carried out and empowered by the grand visions found in Scripture. These visual promises provide hope in times of captivity. As God's people study these Spirit-given images, they lift their eyes in prayer, and they anticipate a coming day of fulfillment. On the approaching horizon of their spiritual vision, rising like the morning sun, a day approaches when sanctuary and city will be forever one. In the midst of a troubled world, our prayer is filled with a holy longing. We yearn with confident expectation when the nations will stream into the temple through the city gates.

In our day, hope is in desperately short supply, because a hope-filled vision of the future is nowhere to be found. Having lost sight of God, the light of His promises no longer shine on the horizon of our lives. All because the world lives "without hope and without God" (Eph. 2:12 NIV). We can get caught up in this darkness and wonder if we are on our own as we labor and pray for church, city, and nation. A cynical voice within whispers, *No one cares, indifference is everywhere, the opposition is just too strong. You are praying and working in vain.*

To help us through the darkness and give us fresh courage, God gives us hope-filled visions that cluster many of His "exceedingly great and precious promises." These are like a "light that shines in a dark place, until the day dawns and the morning star rises in your hearts" (2 Peter 1:4, 19 NKJV). These pictures are more than a prediction of the future, they are God's pledge and vow that He will soon bring to pass all that He promises. They are fuel for mighty prayers to be answered "far more abundantly than all that we ask or think" (Eph. 3:20).

When you sing a refrain from a song and repeat it again and again, you find you can't get it out of your head and it echoes there all day. In a similar way, as you repeatedly meditate on and memorize the Bible's prayer visions, they find their way into the heart fabric of your prayers. You begin to pray with lifted eyes and your heart comes alive with bold and compelling hope. Hope is contagious. The promises within you will certainly flow out to others.

So let's look at some prayer visions God has provided for us through His Word.

GOD'S MULTINATIONAL VISION FOR PRAYER

The first vision we consider is from Isaiah 56. God opened Isaiah's eyes of faith, and the prophet saw streams of foreigners joyfully entering the temple to pray. The gates of the city were ever open. These global guests were invited and ushered in by God himself:

> Foreigners who join themselves to the Lord
>   to minister to him,
> to love the name of the Lord,
>   and to be his servants,
> all who keep the Sabbath without desecrating it and who
>   hold fast my covenant—
> these I will bring to my holy mountain
>   and give them joy in my house of prayer.
> Their burnt offerings and sacrifices
>   will be accepted on my altar;
> for my house shall be called
>   a house of prayer for all nations.
> ISAIAH 56:6–7 NIV

As honored guests, seekers enter the altar court to pray in the very presence of the Almighty. They are not spectators, but with all the sons and daughters of Abraham they enter into joyful and ecstatic prayer fellowship with God's people.

As you pray into this vision, important things happen. You begin to take notice of the immigrants, refugees, and international students who are filling your communities. Putting aside prejudice, you show hospitality and embrace them; it is these very people whom God wants you to invite into His house of prayer. Your heart is moved to prayer by their dislocation, their loneliness and distress, the challenges of raising their children and finding work in a strange, new land. You begin to see migrant workers as individuals, not as part of a nameless crowd.

As you get to know and care for someone from a foreign land, you can ask to pray for them in their presence. Further, you can ask if they would like to know about your prayer life—even if they would like to know how to pray. Often the best gift you can offer to people of other cultures is prayer.

Your prayers will move beyond mere sympathy to compassionate action as you take steps to relieve their distress and loneliness. Open hearts lead to open doors, and you will open your home to welcome them to dine. One of the greatest gifts you can offer your new neighbor is hospitality. The word *hospitality* (philoxenos) literally means "loving the stranger." "Welcoming the stranger and the alien" is one of the oft-repeated commandments of Scripture. Opening our homes and hearts is a clear call to believers (see Rom. 12:13; 1 Tim. 5:10; Heb. 13:2; 1 Peter 4:9).

A VISION OF RENEWAL IN THE INNER CITY

The next prayer vision is from Isaiah 58, in which the prophet foretells the restoration of a broken city lying in rubble, ruined to its very foundations. To rebuild it, the people must offer compassionate, consistent acts of mercy and justice to one another:

> Is not this the fast that I choose:
>> to loose the bonds of wickedness,
>> to undo the straps of the yoke,
> to let the oppressed go free,
>> and to break every yoke?
> Is it not to share your bread with the hungry
>> and bring the homeless poor into your house;
> when you see the naked, to cover him,
>> and not to hide yourself from your own flesh?
> **ISAIAH 58:6–7**

As if deeds of kindness are a prayer, God promises to hear the cry of those who pour out their lives to clothe and shelter others. He reveals Himself to those who serve and pray for the needy and sends them divine power and supply to carry out the work to marvelous completion. God gives those who pray and labor for the needy the unmerited honor of rebuilding the city:

> Then you shall call, and the LORD will answer;
>> you shall cry, and he will say, "Here I am." . . .
> And your ancient ruins shall be rebuilt;
>> you shall raise up the foundations of many generations;
> you shall be called the repairer of the breach,
>> the restorer of streets to dwell in.
> **ISAIAH 58:9, 12**

As we pray this vision of hope for urban renewal, it is already coming to pass! We become what we pray, and God brings to pass what we pray. As someone has said, "Christians are building the show-home so everyone can see what the new neighborhood will look like."

As we pray, God gives us the resolve to go into the broken and rubble-strewn heart of the city and rebuild from the ground up. He gives strength to remove the rock and rubble from the streets, and He gives wisdom to re-lay the foundations. God blesses with perseverance all who pray and labor to bring joy, safety, and hope to the streets of the city.

In many countries, Christians are rebuilding the city. For example, visit the lower east side of Vancouver—Main Street and Hastings Street are its ground zero. This city-center intersection is crowded with panhandlers, addicts, street workers, and the lonely homeless. Spend time prayer walking and getting to know the area and you will find a myriad of churches and inner-city ministries, as well as individual Christians, feeding, praying for, providing counsel and shelter, offering church services, prayer, and Bible study, and otherwise pouring out their lives day after day. The joy and perseverance of these Christian workers are impossible to account for except for their strong trust in a coming day of liberation, and the promised power and love God gives them. As for the people they serve, life on the streets is bitterly difficult, but no one goes hungry, a search for hope and dignity is often rewarded, and a good many become followers of Jesus.

Wherever God's people care for the poor, we find God supplies their needs in amazing ways. As Solomon reminds us, "Whoever is generous to the poor lends to the LORD, and he will repay him for his deed" (Prov. 19:17).

Serving the poor is at the heart of what it means to follow Christ. Paul wrote, "Only. . . remember the poor, the very thing I was eager to do" (Gal. 2:10). If we want God to answer our prayers, we cannot blindly and intentionally walk by those in great need. For example, with a steady stream of generous support, year after year, Serve India feeds, tutors, and cares for thousands of orphans. I have seen it. Hope fills the bright eyes of these children and laughter and joy rise from streets of play.

Augustine connects prayer and helping the poor in a striking image, "If one hopes for one's prayer to take flight to God one must have 'two wings, twin acts of kindness'. . . . one wing is forgiving one's enemy; the other 'wing' is the outstretched hand that gives to the poor."[1]

A CITY IS SECURE WHEN SURROUNDED BY PRAYER

In a third vision, God commends and commands vigilant prayer for the city. He sets forth His mandate in this striking image of watchmen standing guard on the parapets of the holy city:

> On your walls, O Jerusalem,
> I have set watchmen;
> all the day and all the night
> they shall never be silent.
> You who put the Lord in remembrance,
> take no rest,
> and give him no rest
> until he establishes Jerusalem
> and makes it a praise in the earth.
> ISAIAH 62:6–7

In every period of history, God appoints courageous prayer warriors to guard the city. They man the ramparts. They walk the walls. They are ever vigilant and intent on a single purpose. They pray without ceasing for God to guard the city from enemies without and enemies within.

Every believer is called and privileged to "man the ramparts" and intercede for the city they live in. We wonder why so much corruption, violence, and desolation exists in our cities today, but we need look no further than here: the church is failing to guard and keep watch over it through intercessory prayer. The enemy has crept in steadily and now occupies seats of power and propaganda.

When I asked twenty-five Bible school students to raise their hands if they prayed for their city, none put up their hands. Yet they met often to pray for one another. Too often our prayers focus on private and personal concerns, leaving the walls of the city unguarded and open to every vile and harmful influence. There is no greater need in the world today than we cry out to God to raise up a new generation of prayer warriors to guard our cities. No one needs to wait for permission. Even today, any church and every believer can take their post on the wall and cry out for God to bless their city.

THE SPIRIT'S OUTPOURING SAVES MANY AND CLEANSES THE LAND

In terse words, Zechariah's vision summarizes every grand revolution of church revival and urban renewal in history. A God-sized outpouring of Holy Spirit prayer signals the arrival of the kingdom. This movement is pictured in metaphors of a river. Like a waterfall, the spirit of prayer is poured out; as it cascades it forms deep pools and becomes a gushing fountain that brings repentance to everyone that thirsts. As the tide rises and advances, the torrent sweeps away idols and lies:

> I will pour out on the house of David and the inhabitants
> of Jerusalem a spirit of grace and pleas for mercy, so that,
> when they look on me, on him whom they have pierced,

they shall mourn for him, as one mourns for an only child, and weep bitterly over him, as one weeps over a firstborn.... On that day there shall be a fountain opened for the house of David and the inhabitants of Jerusalem, to cleanse them. ... And on that day, declares the LORD of hosts, I will cut off the names of the idols from the land, so that they shall be remembered no more. And also I will remove from the land the prophets and the spirit of uncleanness.

ZECHARIAH 12:10; 13:1–2

We will know the promise of this Scripture is coming to pass when prayer gatherings multiply and tears of sorrow and contrition begin to flow from our prayers. We will know the promise is coming to pass when many are led to Christ, hoping to be washed in the fountain of His blood. They will be cut to the heart and ask, "What shall we do?" And we will respond as Peter did, "Repent and be baptized every one of you in the name of Jesus Christ for the forgiveness of your sins, and you will receive the gift of the Holy Spirit" (Acts 2:38). We will know that the church is truly being revived and that conversions are genuine when personal and cultural idols are exposed, unmasked, and expelled. Hoards of false prophets will disappear simply because people learn to love the truth—even when it cuts deeply—and detest the lies that fill the gossip and propaganda of the city.

Just as we found in the book of Acts, Zechariah's vision of kingdom advance contains a priority and an order.

First, this prophecy of Zechariah motivates us to pray faithfully and patiently, as we ask for God to pour out a spirit of prayer. Waiting prayer begins the flow. Until and unless we wait before Christ in prayer, all other means will utterly fail. The momentum of renewal will be stalled until God's people cry out for the Holy Spirit.

Second, from the headwaters of prayer, an outpouring, cleansing cataract of forgiveness will release to those who weep for their sins, and more and more will bow the knee and convert to the King. The essential evidence that God has poured out the Holy Spirit is when we see a steady flow and increase of sinners coming to faith in Christ.

Third, when prayer and evangelism increase in volume and momentum, the floodtide of salvation and the righteous acts of God's Spirit through His people will surely overwhelm the idols and propaganda that permeate and corrupt the present order.

Zechariah's vision captures the sequence of prayer revival. In every great awakening in the biblical history, and in church history since, we find the order in Zechariah 12:10–13:2 repeated. A spirit of prayer comes first in both sequence and priority. Next follows tearful repentance, spiritual regeneration, and forgiveness, as more and more are saved. Finally, idols and false teachers drown in the river of justice and righteousness.

PRAYER GROWS BY DIVING INTO THE RIVER OF GOD'S SPIRIT

Prayer Current Ministries uses the vision of Ezekiel 47 as the inspiration for our mission. In a grand vision of the promised land, the prophet paints a picture of national renewal. An ever-deepening river flows from the temple and brings healing to the entire nation. We are invited to dive in, go deeper, and learn to navigate its ever-deepening current. We dare not stay on the shore. Read Ezekiel's words:

> Behold, water was issuing from below the threshold of the temple toward the east . . . trickling out on the south side.
> Going on eastward with a measuring line in his hand, the man measured a thousand cubits, and then led me through

the water, and it was ankle-deep. Again he measured a thousand, and led me through the water, and it was knee-deep. Again he measured a thousand, and led me through the water, and it was waist-deep. Again he measured a thousand, and it was a river that I could not pass through, for the water had risen. It was deep enough to swim in, a river that could not be passed through. . . .

Wherever the river goes . . . the waters of the sea . . . become fresh; so everything will live where the river goes. Fishermen will stand beside the sea. . . . It will be a place for the spreading of nets. . . . And on the banks, on both sides of the river, there will grow all kinds of trees for food. Their leaves will not wither, nor their fruit fail, but they will bear fresh fruit every month, because the water for them flows from the sanctuary. Their fruit will be for food, and their leaves for healing.

EZEKIEL 47:1–5, 9–10, 12

In a normal world, the river flows into and through the city. In this vision, the river flows from the city outward. The altar it flows from is positioned at the exact center of the city. It is an eternal spring that wells up from the completed sacrifice of Christ (see John 4:14).

Flowing outward from the altar, this stream deepens and broadens into a river. It begins as a mere trickle, but as it progresses it expands and strengthens because of the inexhaustible springs within.

The swelling and advancing river is a metaphor for the onward progress of God's kingdom from the time of Jesus' sacrifice until today. With unstoppable momentum, the stream pours through history, from generation to generation. As it spreads, its influence deepens, and eventually the whole world will know its life-giving properties. It is the river of the Spirit poured out upon all lands and all nations.

Along the shores of this teeming river are fishermen, diligent and eager to bring in the catch. Clearly, we can connect this to Jesus' words to the disciples, "I will make you fishers of men" (Matt. 4:19).

Step by step, the Spirit invites each of us to enter its flow. He says, *Why are you standing on the shore? Yes, you need to let go of your fears and need to control, but do not fear, I am with you. Now take a big step in and feel the flow. Take another step. Go deeper and feel its power. Now dive in, immerse yourself. Let the current's flow refresh, cleanse, and empower you. Enjoy its healing power.* It is by prayer that we dive in. It is by prayer that we go deeper. It is by prayer that we learn to navigate its current and flow.

WE EXPERIENCE THE GRAND FINALE AND CELEBRATION

Every prayer revolution is fed by the mighty promises and prophecies of Scripture. None is more comprehensive and compelling than the glory-filled promise of Revelation 21. In this powerful vision we come to the fulfillment of the story. The storm subsides and the raging current returns to the steady course, recalling the rivers of Eden, until it covers the whole world and arrives at its final destination. All the streams and tributaries of the biblical narrative and prophecy about church, city, and creation flow into this grand vision of the new and eternal temple, garden city:

> [The angel] carried me away in the Spirit to a great, high mountain, and showed me the holy city Jerusalem coming down out of heaven from God, having the glory of God,

its radiance like a most rare jewel, like a jasper, clear as crystal. It had a great, high wall, with twelve gates, and at the gates twelve angels, and on the gates the names of the twelve tribes of the sons of Israel were inscribed—on the east three gates, on the north three gates, on the south three gates, and on the west three gates. And the wall of the city had twelve foundations, and on them were the twelve names of the twelve apostles of the Lamb.

And the one who spoke with me had a measuring rod of gold to measure the city and its gates and walls. The city lies foursquare, its length the same as its width. And he measured the city with his rod, 12,000 stadia. Its length and width and height are equal. He also measured its wall, 144 cubits by human measurement, which is also an angel's measurement.

REVELATION 21:10–17

To put things in perspective, the New Jerusalem is massive—a thousand times the size of Ezekiel's city—covering an area larger than India. The walls literally reach into the heavens—more than 2,000 kilometers/1,200 miles high and 70 meters/230 feet wide. (For perspective, the Great Wall of China is only six meters/ twenty feet wide.)

This is a living temple city filled with the people of God and is alive with God Himself. Everything within is infused with God. The New Jerusalem pulses and breathes the Spirit-fed worship of God and of the Lamb:

I saw no temple in the city, for its temple is the Lord God the Almighty and the Lamb. And the city has no need of sun or moon to shine on it, for the glory of God gives it light, and its lamp is the Lamb. By its light will the nations walk, and the kings of the earth will bring their glory into it, and its gates will never be shut by day—and there will be no night there. . . .

Then the angel showed me the river of the water of life, bright as crystal, flowing from the throne of God and of the Lamb through the middle of the street of the city; also, on either side of the river, the tree of life with its twelve kinds of fruit, yielding its fruit each month. The leaves of the tree were for the healing of the nations.

REVELATION 21:22–25; 22:1–2

This is the New Jerusalem—a harmonious composite of God's work and human endeavor. The city is transformed into a bride. She is the glorified church, decked out in splendor and arrayed in beauty, eagerly waiting for her husband and King. As the angel told John, "Come, I will show you the Bride, the wife of the Lamb" (Rev. 21:9).

The New Jerusalem is a city and everlasting place of meeting with God: "I saw no temple in the city, for its temple is the Lord God the Almighty and the Lamb" (Rev. 21:22). There is no temple in this city because this city *is* a temple—the ultimate home in which God dwells forever with His people.

This city is made up of many peoples and languages. It is a new world of believers redeemed from every nation: "By its light will the nations walk, and the kings of the earth will bring their glory into it" (Rev. 21:24).

This is the ultimate reward and destiny of Christ's church: the city is creation restored. From the city center, the garden river of paradise is restored and eternally perfected. Nourishment, cleansing, and healing are in its waters. Trees of life bend with fruit for the taking. All the labors of faithful prophets, evangelists, teachers, pastors, and martyrs have contributed to the building of this temple city (see Eph. 4:11–12). No one's work in the Lord has been in vain.

What invincible hope is found in this heavenly picture! This day will arrive soon—in space and time history. It will be a wedding feast of cosmic proportion. The temple and city will forever be one. Every nation will endlessly declare the fame of God. God's church will be victorious and at rest.

All who gaze at this vision and pray for its fulfillment grow bold in prayer with the confident assurance that God's kingdom purposes are even now being fulfilled. Every prayer and act of faith is a brushstroke in the Creator's final and greatest work of art.

In this New Jerusalem, the whole world is reborn—a *palingenesis* of heaven and earth. This is the completed picture and ultimate purpose of Christ, our King. Christ's kingdom has come, is coming, and will come! The day He was born, Jesus' kingdom arrived. His kingdom conquers and advances as His people proclaim Him as King and Savior, and all over the world His kingdom is received and believed. The darkness of sin, idolatry, God haters, and Satan's army are expelled in the unstoppable tide.

THE CENTRAL ROLE OF KINGDOM-COME PRAYER IN REALIZING THIS VISION

We are at the cusp of history and dawning of the eternal age. Our prayers, witness, and good works are like seeds sown in the soil of this broken world, sprouting and growing even now. One day they will bear everlasting fruit. All our labors will be taken up into the heavenly vision. The present history of Christ's church and the earth itself are not futile scraps to be discarded in the coming age. All things in heaven and earth are being reconciled and will be finally reconciled in Christ (see Eph. 1:9–10). Not only will heaven come down to earth (Rev. 21:2), earth will be taken up into heaven. All that is silver and gold will remain, including the obedient works of God's faithful people; faith, hope, and love will remain and all else will perish (see 1 Cor. 3:12–15; 13:13).

Today's prayer revolution is fed by God's great promises embedded in the visions of Scripture. As we unite in earnest prayer, these visions transform from inspiring pictures to imperative sermons. However, we do not start at the finish line. We advance one step at a time. (See Appendix A, where we chart proven practices to engage in a prayer revolution.) As we learned in the last chapter, church revival and urban renewal are measured in decades. Years of patient and persistent prayer and prayer training are essential in order to make disciples through prayer. To become a house of prayer, a praying leader, or a leader in prayer involves an intentional plan to make disciples through prayer. Our prayer is to this end: "Lord, raise up men and women not only who fulfil their calling in prayer, but who give their lives to serving the church and keeping watch over the city, who put the Lord in remembrance, taking no rest and giving You no rest until You establish the Jerusalem of our day a praise in all the earth" (see Isa. 62:6–7).

Every revolution is fed by a compelling revelation of a hoped-for future. This vision can be conceived and discussed by selected leaders. However, the real movement and momentum happen when the proletariat, a multitude of ordinary people, enact the vision in their homes, neighborhoods, and workplaces. God is raising up leaders to initiate movements of prayer, but the proof that a prayer revolution is underway will be when many thousands of believers unite in hundreds of gatherings to cry out to our ascended King to save and heal our land.

The reason why communism, national socialism, feminism,

environmentalism, or any other global movement changes the world is that everyone dives in—everyone puts heart and hands into the realization of the vision. Sheer social pressure makes it a joy to enlist and a shame to be indifferent or uninvolved. When the revolution is in full swing, indifference is treason, abandoning the cause is desertion.

God is calling His people to enlist in His vision to make a new world. When God calls, there can be no bystanders or spectators. Take up the cause. Pray and then pray some more. Unite with others to pray. Let the promise of seeing God work, and the swelling tide of joy, sweep you into His revolution of prayer.

Kingdom-Come Prayer Today

1. We become what we pray. How can we pray into these visions?

2. We are called to build a house of prayer. How many "foreigners" are there in your community? In what ways can you open the doors of the church to let them stream in?

3. What will it look like if God fulfills Isaiah 58 and uses you to be a minister of justice and a rebuilder of ancient walls?

4. Pray the sequence in Zechariah, first personally and then on behalf of the church.

5. Big visions require big prayers. The vision in Revelation 21 is the biggest vision of all. It calls for mighty prayers of faith. What are some ways you can pray into this vision?

Ten Steps Forward:

HOW TO IMPLEMENT KINGDOM PRAYER FOR CHURCH AND CITY

Through a simple prayer in a monastery garden, I was converted at the age of seventeen. Soon after I traveled to Denmark, the land of my ancestors, and from Denmark I went to Switzerland and skied until I exhausted my limited resources.

Before I headed to Europe, I attended my first Christian concert at my high school. I talked with the band leader afterward, and he encouraged me to visit the international headquarters of Youth for Christ in Geneva during my travels. I agreed and when I got there I was sure they would point me to some great gospel work I could pursue in a remote destination. Instead they pointed me up the Swiss Alps to a little community called L'Abri.

This was my first encounter with prayer as a way of life. The Christian community of L'Abri embodied prayer. Every Monday morning we gathered to pray for two hours. Before and after each meal we prayed meaty prayers. Leaders enveloped their teachings with prayer. A good number came to attend Sunday evening prayer meetings. House leaders set aside one day each month for extended prayer and fasting. And I joined a group of young men who were schooled in prayer practices.

The presence of God was an unquestionable reality. The fellowship in prayer often broke our hearts with affection for God and one another. A sense of purpose pervaded each day and each meeting. People were birthed into Christ, and they were birthed into prayer.

Over the years, others have taught me to pray, either expressly or by example (Jack Miller and Archie Parrish among them).

The following "steps forward" in kingdom prayer narrate practices I have learned from others, received at L'Abri, or administered at Grace Church Vancouver. These steps forward embody some of our prayer practices and principles over the past thirty years of bringing kingdom prayer into the artery of churches and cities.

These steps forward are not a recipe for prayer. Nor are they a formula. No "prayer plan" guarantees kingdom advance and expansion. Rather, the delights of prayer are its individual, organic, spontaneous, and combustive elements. As each person prays, he discovers for himself new joys in the adventure of following Christ in a living way. When one learns to wait upon God in prayer, she discovers fresh wisdom and timely insight hitherto unknown. To mimic any strategy guarantees a stale, secondhand approach.

At the same time, while avoiding formulas and illusions of silver-bullet solutions, there are proven practices to aid our prayer commitment. As long as these approaches are simply "training wheels," they can be very helpful.

Step 1: Form Your Plans in Prayer

First, take God at His Word that He will let you in on His plan for your life and mission. As Proverbs 16:3 says, "Commit your work to the LORD, and your plans will be established."

In prayer, learn to live supernaturally. You will receive just-in-time revelations of His call and purpose as you read His Word, letting the word of Christ dwell richly within, and wait in prayer. May God give you the spirit of wisdom and revelation in the knowledge of Him, having the eyes of your heart enlightened (see Eph. 1:17–18).

Listening to God and partnering with Him was Jesus' method and should be ours:

> The Son can do nothing of his own accord, but only what he sees the Father doing. For whatever the Father does, that the Son does likewise. For the Father loves the Son and shows him all that he himself is doing. And greater works than these will he show him, so that you may marvel.
> JOHN 5:19–20

Have personal and corporate days of "prayer and planning," engaging with God in a rhythm of prayer, the Word, and sharing.

Step 2: Build a Prayer-Centered Church and Mission by Keeping Prayer at the Center Flowing Outward

Bring people to prayer. Call people to specific gatherings and seasons of prayer, such as prayer meetings, prayer vigils, fasting and prayer, and prayer-training opportunities.

Just as important: bring prayer to the people so that prayer is increased among people in every area—where prayer acts as a lifeblood that permeates and animates every aspect of mission and ministry. Train every leader to lead their people and ministry area in prayer (see steps 6 and 7).

This leads to a praying church who exudes a praying culture, where every person is engaged in prayer no matter what their current commitment to prayer is—whether a newcomer on Sunday at the hospitality table or prayer altar after service, to a small group member during Bible study, to a key leader during a planning meeting.

We use the diagram below to illustrate an important truth that prayer meetings are only one way among many to gather people to prayer. In fact, it is easier and has a longer-term effect when prayer is inserted into existing meetings and ministries. Train leaders in each area of mission and ministry to lead in prayer and facilitate the prayer of others and the entire body will light up with intercession for the church and its mission.

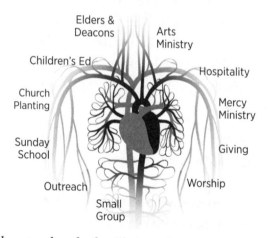

Though not a church, the Christian human-rights group International Justice Mission (IJM) sets a powerful example for the church of weaving habits of prayer into their daily practices. Leaders lead from the knees as they follow their mission strategy—"The work of justice begins in prayer"—and practice what they preach. Each staff member gets the first thirty minutes of their workday for silence, prayer, meditation, and spiritual reflection. IJM also gathers their staff for thirty minutes of daily corporate prayer, in addition to hosting quarterly offsite spiritual retreats and providing employees with an annual day for private spiritual retreat.

One national church-planting network has implemented a daily prayer for mission advance by setting their cellphone alarms at 10:02 as a call to prayer. This reminds them throughout their days of Luke 10:2, to "pray earnestly to the Lord of the harvest to send out laborers into his harvest."

We live in a disconnected and busy world so it is hard to bring people to prayer meetings. It makes more sense to take prayer meetings to people. By inserting prayer into the existing flow of life and mission, we deepen our fellowship in Christ and multiply our intercession.

Step 3: Move Prayer Meetings from Boredom to Adventure

Prayer meetings can quickly become stagnant, monotonous, and vulnerable to poor attendance. You can keep vibrant kingdom prayer fresh by keeping prayer clusters small—only two to four people.

Encourage participants to pray briefly but often; the acronym ABC (audible, brief, conversational and Christ-centered) is a helpful guide.

Begin the prayer time with reading a brief Scripture passage and then practicing the Goal of Thirds: one-third instruction, one-third interaction, one-third intercession. For one example, if you have thirty minutes to lead a study, start the first ten minutes by having someone read a brief inspiring passage. You may add a few brief comments on why you chose the passage for this time. Then pray or have people pray on their own. For the next ten minutes, break larger meetings into groups of three. Provide a practical, heart-worthy question for them to discuss. After five minutes encourage them to pray what they have learned for one another. For the last ten minutes, solicit insights from a few people, then ask people to pray for church or personal requests.

GOAL OF THIRDS

Turn every meeting into a prayer meeting by applying the Goal of Thirds. Bringing prayer into the agenda of every meeting transforms them by the presence of Jesus—bringing unity to divided agendas in board meetings, hope to hospital visitations, heart transformation to Sunday school lessons.

Turn every conversation into one that actively invites God in. Model and practice "on the spot" prayer in all settings. This will help people get used to praying with anyone anytime. Instead of saying, "I will pray for you," say, "May I pray for you now?"

Step 4: Practice Corporate Embodiments of Prayer

Praying with others is supremely helpful. Vision for God's kingdom germinates in the soil of concerted, united prayer. Corporate prayer is the soil in which vision from God grows from mustard seed to mighty plant, providing shade and shelter for many.

Moreover, we need to learn to "embody" our prayers: to stand up or kneel, raise hands, speak out loud, gather in groups and pray in a circle. These are some of the many ways to move prayer from interior to exterior, from head to heart, from church to city.

Step 5: Incorporate Prayer Walking into Spiritual Rhythms

By far, one of the most important "prayer embodiments" is prayer walking. As you walk the streets of your neighborhood or city, you begin to see things from Jesus' perspective.

One creative example of prayer walking involved mission leaders who arranged a one-day prayer walk of the entire metroplex of Miami, Florida. This group of leaders rode the train from north to south Miami, stopping at every major station along the way to form a prayer circle. A leader from each area narrated the needs and opportunities of that community, pointing out essential landmarks and institutions. In this way, they prayed for the specific neighborhoods of the entire city in detail and "on location."

When you prayer walk your community, you will discover a new vision and concern for its people and places.

Step 6: Choose Leaders Who Are Committed to Prayer and Train Them to Pray

We become what we pray. Choose, appoint, elect, or hire people who are excited to be part of a praying team. Before long, prayer will advance and inform the entire culture of your enterprise.

When examining potential leaders, spend as much time exploring their prayer life and practices as their proficiency in teaching and pastoring. Ask about their personal prayer practices. Ensure that all nominees for office take a basic training prayer course before being placed before the congregation for voting.

Prayer will be pushed to the margins unless recognized officers and leaders provide the example of a godly life of intercession for the church and world. Choose your strongest leaders to train others in prayer.

Likewise, train your congregational prayer leaders how to lead in prayer, so that public prayer projects weight and meaning rather than just a laundry list of health problems and news-related issues. Leading with the Lord's Prayer or other psalm or Scripture ensures the vitality of congregational prayer.

Make sure to provide basic prayer training before asking someone to lead in prayer, just as you would if asking someone to teach or lead a Bible study. Debrief prayer leadership just as you would debrief a sermon or Bible study.

Another important way to multiply prayer leadership and to care for the flock is to implement prayer visitation. Train several leaders and leader couples in how to minister to the members of a flock in prayer. The apostle Paul provides a stellar example of ministering in prayer, as he prayed sixty-four times for the churches (see chapter 6). The time-honored practice of regular elder visitation can be updated by sending a mature couple to pray for each household. Whenever an individual, couple, or family is going through hard times, send a team to pray for them.

Step 7: Train Small Group Leaders to Be Prayer Leaders

When the ethos of small groups embodies vibrant prayer, every meeting becomes a prayer meeting, and organic prayer begins to form the bedrock of your church. Every small group leader can be trained to become a prayer leader.

Provide small groups the pattern of equal parts fellowship, study, and prayer. At Grace Vancouver Church we encouraged people to enjoy dinner together, then move into a season of praise and thanksgiving, followed by a brief Bible study, with lots of discussion and application.

The stage is thus set for informed prayer for others and for one another. In order to balance inward and outward concerns, the prayer time begins with praying for the church and the city. After this we field personal requests and pray for one another.

Step 8: Implement Seasons of "Waiting Prayer" into the Calendar

By "waiting prayer" I mean designated seasons of prayer and fasting, similar to the first disciples' waiting for the promised Holy Spirit as Jesus commanded them. In the case of Grace Vancouver, we started with sixteen weeks of prayer meetings. Once the church began, we continued to gather weekly for two hours of prayer and reporting.

Three times a year (and even now at Prayer Current), we held a day of prayer and fasting, and every fall we gathered all our ministry leaders together for a day of prayer and planning. These prayer times were not only times of preparation; they were highpoints of spiritual joy and team building. Everyone gets to pray and everyone gets a say. This is a proven recipe for long-term bonds of trust and deep fellowship.

Step 9: Form Prayer Evangelism Triads

To encourage people in personal mission and evangelism, establish a network of prayer-evangelism triads, in which each participant chooses three non-Christian friends or neighbors to pray for. Triads gather regularly to pray for one another's lives and outreach. Each person in the triad shares according to three questions to focus prayers:

1. How are you growing in your prayer friendship with Jesus?
2. How are you connecting with your unbelieving friends and neighbors in acts of kindness and words of wisdom?
3. How can we best pray for them, and for your opportunities to love and serve them?

Once the group has strong cohesion and clear purpose, one or two members will leave to form a new triad. The goal is to have every member and faithful attender become part of a prayer triad. The original group members keep in touch with one another to maintain friendship and encourage the process.

Step 10: Discover and Adopt Mottos for Prayer Advance

Over the years, Prayer Current has assembled a collection of mottos that inspire us to prioritize prayer and to instill an ongoing culture of kingdom prayer. Here are some of our favorites:

We are what we pray.
We become what we pray.
We either pray it open or we pry it open.
There is no cruise control with prayer.
Pray or be prey.
We do not pray for revival. Prayer is revival.
Spiritual warfare does not follow prayer. Prayer is spiritual warfare.

As in all things, pray about how God wants you to lead and grow as you endeavor in kingdom prayer.

A PRAYER GRID TO BUILD THE COMING KINGDOM

Here is a simple sequence of prayer as a way to focus on each portion of the Lord's Prayer. Pray through one priority in the prayer grid (i.e. one column) at a time from top to bottom. Take, for example, praying through the first pattern and priority: God as Father.

1. Upward (Pattern and Priority)

- Start your prayer by focusing on the priority upward to God, always beginning by acknowledging God as Father.
- Praise Jesus for the priority, for adoption as sons and daughters into God's family.
- Meditate on the priority of being a child of God. Ask the Holy Spirit to show you what it means. What does the priority, this reality, tell you about God?

2. Inward (Passions)

- Next pray the priority, the truth of your identity, *into your heart*. Talk with God about it.
- How is the priority *growing or lacking* in your heart and life?

3. Outward (People)

- *What will your life look like* as this priority takes deeper root, as you acknowledge and know God to be Father? Ask Jesus to *transform your heart* and life to be more like His.
- Now pray for *others to experience more of God's* promises and priority in their lives and that they would come to know Him as Father.
- Pray for *the world, the church, and the city,* especially as needs relate to the priority at hand.

4. Upward (Praise)

- End by *praising God* for His blessings and answers to prayer. *Recognize* how God has been present. *Thank* Him.

For further elaboration on using this prayer sequence/grid, see *Seven Days of Prayer with Jesus* by John Smed from www.prayer-current.com.

PATTERN	Our **Father** in heaven	**Hallowed** be your name	Your **kingdom** come	**Your will** be done, on earth as it is in heaven	Give us this day our **daily bread**	**Forgive us** our debts, as we also have forgiven our debtors	**Lead us** not into temptation, but deliver us from evil
PRIORITY & PROMISE	Relationship Prayer	Worship	Evangelism City renewal	Mercy Social justice	Contentment Generosity Simplicity	Unity Reconciliation	Guidance Advance
Pray God's **PASSIONS** into my own heart							
Pray God's blessing for other **PEOPLE**							
PRAISE for who He is & thank Him for answers to prayers							

A PRAYER FOR THE HEART OF YOUR NATION (OR CITY)

There are practical ways you can encourage intercession for your land. One way to pray effectively is to gather in groups of up to twelve and pray for the nation (or you can divide up according to city neighborhoods) in the same way you pray for a person. In New York City, for example, we divided fifty attendees into six groups—one for each borough and one for Manhattan. When we met with a team of campus workers who ministered in several universities, we simply divided those attending into the six or seven leaders for each city they worked in.

As you pray, create a flip chart and divide it into four quadrants. In each corner write one of these four questions:

LOVE: What do you love about your country?	**LAMENT:** What do you lament about your nation?
REPENT: What idols and sins grieve you (and God) about your country?	**RESPOND:** How can we pray for her and serve her?

Next, have the group discuss and write down their answers to these questions.

• **For quadrant one,** think and pray about why you love the nation where God has placed you (see Acts 17:26–28) and write down your answers.

For instance, you may write: Work-life balance. Beauty of nature and environmental sustainability. Diversity, open-minded, multicultural. Community development. Spiritual. Seeking for purpose/good. Medical and welfare for those in need.

• **For quadrant two,** discussing the hurts and brokenness, consider the different ways Satan and sin are wounding and oppressing.

For instance, you may write: Hyper-sexualized; drug trade

and human trafficking. Absence of God, therefore of hope; secular desert, unbelief, distraction, superficiality, individualism, self-worship leading to loneliness, disconnection and alienation. Mental health struggles, addictions. Poverty, disparity of wealth, inflated unaffordable housing.

- **In the third quadrant,** write down the nation's sins and the idols that will bring judgment if not repented of.

For instance, you may write: Idols to confess: pleasure, comfort, leisure approval, acceptance, tolerance. Greed, money, materialism. Self (reliance, glorification, worship).

- **In the fourth quadrant,** write down the prayers and actions God is calling you to enact for your land.

You may write: Jesus gave up all pleasure of heaven, approval of His Father, and submitted to the cross for us to receive ultimate riches and approval. Speak God's story; art and film outreach. Creation care, outdoor ministries. Social justice, serving the poor, practicing hospitality. Prayer evangelism.

Once the chart is complete, have the group take an extended period to pray one quadrant at a time. The entire process should take less than an hour.

If you have a larger number joining you in prayer, divide the group into teams of five to eight, then let each group fill out the quadrants and pray for the country. After each team is finished praying, pass the sheet on to the next group, or have the groups walk around the room to different tables, so you can see how others care about their country—and pray again.

Of course, if several nations are represented, all the better! You can pray for countries around the world this way. Circumnavigate the globe through kingdom prayer!

You can also use this exercise to pray for cities, neighborhoods, and people groups.

Select Bibliography

Beeke, Joel R., and Brian G. Najapfour, editors. *Taking Hold of God: Reformed and Puritan Perspectives on Prayer.* Grand Rapids, MI: Reformation Heritage/Soli Deo Gloria, 2011.

Bloesch, Donald G. *The Struggle of Prayer.* Colorado Springs, CO: Helmers & Howard, 1988.

Carson, D. A., editor. *Teach Us to Pray: Prayer in the Bible and the World.* Eugene, OR: Wipf and Stock, 2002.

Hand, Thomas A. *Saint Augustine on Prayer.* Pine Beach, NJ: Newman House Press, 1963.

Hayes, Dan. *Fireseeds of Spiritual Awakening.* Orlando, FL: Cru Press, 2009.

Houston, James. *The Transforming Friendship: A Guide to Prayer.* Vancouver: Regent Press, 2010.

Jeffrey, David Lyle, editor. *A Burning and a Shining Light: English Spirituality in the Age of Wesley,* 3rd ed. Vancouver: Regent Press, 2006.

Keller, Timothy. *Center Church: Doing Balanced, Gospel-Centered Ministry in Your City.* Grand Rapids, MI: Zondervan, 2012.

McIntyre, David. *The Hidden Life of Prayer: The Life-blood of the Christian.* Plantation, FL: Fowler Digital Books, 2010. Originally published in 1891.

Murray, Andrew. *The Ministry of Intercession.* Bloomington, MN: Bethany House, 2003.

Spurgeon, Charles. *The Power of Prayer in a Believer's Life.* Lynwood, WA. Emerald Books, 1993.

Acknowledgments

Many thanks to Anne Husak and Renee Reynolds for their tireless and generous help in putting the chapters of the book into presentable form.

I want to share my appreciation for Ginger Kolbaba, who persisted, shaped, prodded, and otherwise energized the editing process to help me make a more readable and applicable manuscript.

A special thanks to Brandon O'Brien and Duane Sherman, who share the same passion for prayer and who opened the door for *Prayer Revolution* to be published.

Notes

The World Awaits a Prayer Revolution
1. Ed Stetzer and Daniel Im, *Multiplication Today, Movements Tomorrow: Practices, Barriers, and an Ecosystem* (Nashville: New Churches and Lifeway Research, 2016), 40.
2. Charles Haddon Spurgeon, "The Lover of God's Law Filled with Peace," preached on January 22, 1888, from *The Tabernacle Metropolitan Pulpit*, Volume 34, accessed October 17, 2019, https://www.spurgeon.org/resource-library/sermons/the-lover-of-gods-law-filled-with-peace#flipbook/.
3. https://www.prayercurrent.com/.

Chapter 1: The King Comes in Prayer
1. Rick Doyle Founds, "Lord, I Lift Your Name on High," ©1989 Marantha! Music.

Chapter 2: The King's Strategy for Prayer
1. Quoted in Thomas A. Hand, *Augustine on Prayer* (Totowa, NJ: Catholic Book Publishing, 1986), 35.
2. Tertullian, "The Spiritual Offering of Prayer," from *On Prayer* by Tertullian, in *The Liturgy of the Hours*, https://homewoodcpc.org/category/daily-devotional/year-1-2018-2019/lent-year-1/3rd-week-in-lent/.

Chapter 3: The King's Passion for a House of Prayer
1. This rejection of those outside was confirmed elsewhere in the New Testament history. Rather than welcoming the nations, Gentile worshipers were treated as tainted. Jewish worshipers were prohibited from touching or even talking with foreigners lest they become unclean (see Acts 10:27–28).
2. Romans 11 narrates God's future and full intent for the nation of Israel.
3. *Voice of the Martyrs* is a monthly magazine and a great resource to aid our prayers in this regard.
4. *Thirty Days of Prayer for the Muslim World* is a prayer program with a thirty-day guide, which is accessible at https://www.30daysprayer.com/. Millions of Christians are now praying for thirty days during Ramadan. *Perspectives on World Mission* is the text for a course offered at many churches. The *Kairos* course is an abbreviated version

that can help any believer become a "world Christian."

5. Evan Wiggs, "Moravian Revival," Measure of Gold Revival Ministries, accessed October 25, 2019, http://www.evanwiggs.com/revival/history/moravian.html; see also Edward Rondthaler, quoted in John Greenfield, *Power from On High*, ed. Mark Mirza (Atlanta: CTM, 2017), 21; John Greenfield, *Power from On High: The 200th Anniversary of the Great Moravian Revival, 1727–1927*, accessed October 25, 2019, https://www.gospeltruth.net/moravian.htm.

6. "Moravian Pentecost," Women of Christianity, May 16, 2011, http://womenofchristianity.com/page/331/.

7. Leslie K. Tarr, "A Prayer Meeting That Lasted 100 Years," *Christian History*, 1982, https://www.christianitytoday.com/history/issues/issue-1/when-asked-his-reasons-for-going-to-st-thomas-leonard.html?id=3263&number=9&type=issuePrev.

8. Evan Wiggs, "Moravian Revival," Measure of Gold Revival Ministries, accessed October 25, 2019, http://www.evanwiggs.com/revival/history/moravian.html; Robert Hill, "7. Topical Prayer: Testimonial," Bible.org, May 11, 2004, https://bible.org/seriespage/topical-prayer-testimonial.

Chapter 4: How Christ's Ascension Brings a New Day for Prayer

1. *The London Telegram* estimates the number at 58 million, October 18, 2019.

2. Tony Lambert, *China's Christian Millions* (New York: Monarch Books, 2006), 233.

3. David Garrison, *A Wind in the House of Islam* (Monument, CO: Wigtake Resource, 2014), 5.

4. *Thirty Days of Prayer for the Muslim World* keep a running count on their home page. More than 1.6 million people have used their prayer guide alone.

5. Garrison, *A Wind in the House of Islam*, 5.

Chapter 5: How Holy Spirit Advances Ignite in Prayer

1. Adapted from John Smed, "Prayer and the Sequence of New Testament Mission," OnMovements.com, https://onmovements.com/?p=59.

Chapter 6: How Prayer Fuels a Global Movement

1. See the research in David Garrison, *A Wind in the House of Islam*, 5.

2. https://www.opendoorsusa.org/christian-persecution/.

3. Ibid.

4. "Christian Persecution 'At Near Genocide Levels'," BBC News, May 3, 2019, https://www.bbc.com/news/uk-48146305.

Chapter 7: How Prayer Brings Urban Renewal

1. From a talk he gave and I attended.

2. "Lead On, O King Eternal" by Ernest Shurtleff, copyright © 1888, public domain.

3. Lex Loizides, "A Prayer Meeting that Changed the World," *Christian History Review*, August 14, 2009, https://lexloiz.wordpress.com/2009/08/14/a-prayer-meeting-that-changed-the-world/.

4. David Lyle Jeffrey, ed., *A Burning and Shining Light: English Spirituality in the Age of Wesley* (Grand Rapids, MI: Eerdmans, 1987), 21.

5. Societal reform following awakenings is gradual. Like leaven, it starts small and takes

time, but before long penetrates the whole. For instance, William Wilberforce's emancipation directive occurred nearly a century after that first outpouring (from 1739 to 1833). And though George Whitefield would one day raise support to build orphanages in Georgia, he also justified keeping slaves to do the work. This blemish on his record reveals how the evangelical conscience had not yet developed to its later maturity. John Wesley himself was utterly opposed to slavery. It remained for later evangelicals, such as John Newton and his disciple William Wilberforce, as well as David Livingstone, the great explorer and missionary to Africa, to champion the abolition movement and bring it to a final close.

6. Jeffrey, *A Burning and Shining Light*, 21.

Chapter 8: How a Nation Is Renewed Through Repentance

1. See Ezra 9, Nehemiah 9, and Daniel 9 as models for how these righteous leaders prayed corporately for their nation.

2. Ernest W. Shurtleff, "Lead On, O King Eternal," copyright © 1888, public domain.

3. Angus Reid, "Religion, Faith, and the Public Square," March 26, 2015, http://angus-reid.org/religion-faith-public-square/.

4. Frank Newport, "In U.S., Four in Ten Report Attending Church in Last Week," Gallup, December 24, 2013, https://news.gallup.com/poll/166613/four-report-attending-church-last-week.aspx.

5. Jeffrey M. Jones, "U.S. Church Membership Down Sharply in Past Two Decades," Gallup, April 18, 2019, https://news.gallup.com/poll/248837/church-membership-down-sharply-past-two-decades.aspx.

6. Joanna Smith, "Trudeau Liberals Continue to Ask Applicants for Summer Job Funds Their View on Abortion," *National Post*, April 29, 2019, https://nationalpost.com/news/canada/feds-denied-summer-job-grants-to-26-groups-over-abortion-rights-issue.

7. Kathleen Harris, "Number of Canadians Choosing Medically Assisted Death Jumps 30 Percent," CBC News, June 21, 2018, https://www.cbc.ca/news/politics/maid-assisted-death-increase-1.4715944.

8. R. Cargill, "A Goodly Heritage, (45): The Welsh Revival of 1904-05" *Believer's Magazine*, October 2016, http://www.believersmagazine.com/bm.php?i=20161003.

9. William T. Stead, G. Campbell Morgan, et al, *The Welsh Revival & The Story of The Welsh Revival by Eyewitnesses* (Lawton, OK: Trumpet Press, 2015), 117–8.

10. David Matthews, *I Saw the Welsh Revival* (Pensacola, FL: Christian Life Books, 2002), np.

11. J. Edwin Orr, *Evangelical Awakenings in Latin America* (Bloomington, MN: Bethany Fellowship, 1978), 41.

Chapter 9: How Idols Are Removed Through Kingdom Prayer

1. "The Future of World Religions," Pew-Templeton Global Religious Futures Project (Washington: Pew Research Center, 2016), http://www.globalreligiousfutures.org/.

2. John Bunyan, *The Pilgrim's Progress* (London: High Holborn, 1837), 151.

3. Ibid., 152–53.

4. Half of Jesus' parables (sixteen out of thirty-eight, to be exact) warned about the lure

and destructiveness of riches. Moreover, it is indeed sobering that Jesus called out those who hated Him and who would mastermind His crucifixion as "lovers of money."

5. Madeleine Delbrêl, *We, the Ordinary People of the Streets*, trans. David Louis Schindler Jr. and Charles F. Mann (Grand Rapids, MI: W.B. Eerdmans, 2000), 20.

Chapter 10: How Exiles Are Sustained Through Regenerating Prayer

1. *Calvin's Institutes: A New Compend*, Hugh T. Kerr, ed. (Louisville, KY: Westminster John Knox, 1989), 108.

2. For instance, see Nick Miroff, "Cuba Undergoes a Religious Revival," *The Guardian*, June 12, 2015, https://www.theguardian.com/world/2015/jun/12/cuba-religious-revival-christian-denominations.

Chapter 11: How a Church Is Revived and a City Is Renewed Through Prayer

1. Chart adapted from *The Ryrie NASB Study Bible* (Chicago: Moody Publishers, 2012), 547, 561.

2. Quoted in William Garden Blaikie, *The Personal Life of David Livingstone* (London: John Murray, 1881), 162.

Conclusion: Praying the Spirit's Vision

1. William Harmless, *Augustine and the Catachumenate* (Collegeville, MN: Liturgical Press, 1995, 2014), 344.

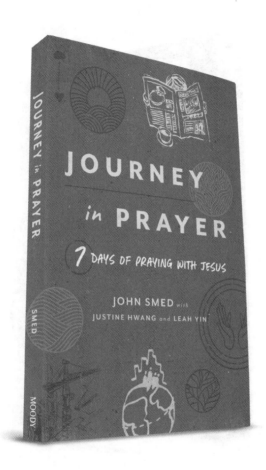